The Allotme k

A guide to promoting an   e

Sophie Andrews

eco-logic books

First published in 2001 by eco-logic books
Second Edition 2005

ISBN   1 899233 10 5

Cartoons and cover design: **Kate Evans**

Additional Cartoons: **Natascha Arsalan**
Pete Loveday

Design & Typesetting: **Steve Palmer**

Printing & Binding: **Russell Press**

Further copies of the book can be purchased from:

eco-logic books

10 -12 Picton St, Bristol, BS6 5QA, England

Telephone: 0117 942 0165

Fax: 0117 942 0164

email: books@eco-logicbooks.com

web: www.eco-logicbooks.com

eco-logic books produce a mail order catalogue of books that promote practical solutions to environmental problems, sustainable development, permaculture and related topics. A FREE copy of this catalogue can be downloaded from their website.

Disclaimer: Whilst every effort has been made to ensure the accuracy of the information in this book the publisher and author accept no responsibility for any errors or omissions.

ACKNOWLEDGEMENTS

Most books are written using other books as sources of information. This book relied upon practical advice from people actually doing it. I could not have written a word without the help of other experts and activists in the field (or on the plot). Most of those people appear in the contacts list, and are quoted directly in these pages. So many people have helped in the making of this book that it has been difficult to keep track – thank you to everyone.

Particular thanks for support, ideas, and information, are due to:

Steve Clampin,	Bristol City Council
Richard Clare,	Sheffield Organic Food Initiative
Jenny Cottee,	Tilehurst Allotments
Ian Egginton-Metters,	Federation of City Farms and Community Gardens
Charlie Hopkins,	Earthrights Solicitors
John Smyth,	Brighton and Hove Allotments Federation
Bethan Stagg,	ARI
Shelagh Wilson,	Hastings and St Leonard's Allotment Federation
Chris Carver	
Mark Jackson	
George Monbiot	
P. Neckie	
Mario Rozanski	
Andy Sabel	
Martin Stott	
and everyone at The Land Is Ours.	

Parts of the Planning chapter are reproduced from The Land Is Ours pamphlet, An Activist's Guide to the Planning System, by **Richard Moyse**. Additional thanks go to **Chris Maile**, Campaign for Planning Sanity, for crucial amendments and additions to Chapters 6 and 7.

I affirme, (and I challenge you to disprove) that the earth was made to be a common Treasury of livelihood for all, without respect of persons, and was not made to be bought and sold.

Gerrard Winstanley, 1649

CONTENTS

Foreword

The 20th century could fairly be described as the century of monoculture. Over the past 100 years, much of the great diversity of wildlife, landuse, architecture and human culture which made the world such an extraordinary and engaging place has been pushed aside and replaced with a single way of life. Key resources have been enclosed and monopolised by corporations. Land which once answered many human needs – food, shelter, water, medicine, fibres, grazing, fuel, leisure, peace, remembrance and worship – has been forced instead to answer only one: profit. The most efficient means of making money is to select the most lucrative product and concentrate on producing that. Anything which answers other needs is dismissed as inefficient, and burnt, ploughed, fenced, drained, flooded or concreted over.

The century of monoculture has left us with a world lacking in texture. Monoculture has a polished surface, one on which we constantly slip when we try to engage with it. Bleak housing estates, giant superstores, ringroads and motorways, wheatfields stretching to the horizon, concrete reservoirs and industrial parks surrounded by security fences don't reflect our scale, the human scale, but quite another: the profit scale. We find it hard to attach ourselves to these landscapes, to put down roots, as there is so little to cling on to. The grain of life has been polished away. Monoculture is economically efficient only in direct proportion to its social inefficiency.

Allotments are among the few remaining places in Britain in which the grain of life is still visible. Crafted by the hands and hoes of generations of hard-working people, theirs is by definition a human scale; irregular, idiosyncratic and inconsistent, a last line of defence against the stiff brush of sanitary sameness. They are among the few places which make our towns and cities, even our countryside (where agro-industry has swept away everything else) habitable, for both humans and wildlife. Most importantly, they belong to us, not to corporations, agribusinessmen, aristocrats or property developers. In this increasingly privatised world, they are among the last vestiges of the common property (tempered by rights of usufruct) which once governed human relations in most parts of the planet, and which ensured that nearly everyone had a fair share of the wealth of the earth.

To the developers who have taken everything else from us, allotments represent a source of potential profit, a chance to replace inefficient multiculture with lucrative monoculture. They will seize them as they have seized so many other community assets, unless we fight unrelentingly to keep them in the common domain. If we are to win this fight, we must, as Sophie Andrews shows, be creative, rather than simply reactive. We must demonstrate the importance of allotments to generations who have been forcibly deprived of contact with diversity, who, unable to inhabit the polished world they have been bequeathed, have taken refuge instead in virtual worlds, where they can find, if nothing else, a diversity of imagination. We must show the people who oversee development that the value of these places cannot be represented on a balance sheet. We must help the people who cherish allotments to find new ways of keeping them out of the hands of the enemies of community life.

Sophie Andrews has emerged as the radical voice the allotments movement has long required. Her efforts will help us to make the 21st century a century of restoration, allowing us once more to engage with the grain of life, to rebuild a world which belongs to us, a world fit for human beings to inhabit.

George Monbiot

Introduction

Allotments are right under our noses, yet many of us don't know anything about them. We don't know who owns them or how to rent one; we don't know how to garden, or where to go for help and advice. Many people see allotments as old-fashioned and anachronistic, sidelined by councils and government, lost within old and vague laws. At the same time allotment land is always under threat from developers. Allotment Associations vary in effectiveness from the vibrant and exciting to those that exist in name only.

Recently there has been much talk about environmentally sustainable cities. Many of us want to live healthier lives, connected to the land and to nature. With the growth of the green movement, we are beginning to see that we can and must do things very differently to be sustainable. We are in the process of reinventing ourselves and our lives, taking many of the ways of doing things from the past, and adding new ideas and processes. Allotments should be part of our plans for a more sustainable future.

Unlike many cities and towns globally we are lucky that we have access to land – allotments, the vestiges of common land – and this widens our sense of belonging, of community. The benefits which sustainable communities bring outweighs the price of the land in which they are rooted. We need to convince government and developers that paying lip service to environmental sustainability is not enough, that economic gain is less important than retaining that land and building strong neighbourhoods.

Many of the ideas in this book are designed to make you think and organise in different ways. However, the world is changing and new ideas come and go. Experience shows that it will take longer still for government policy and legislation to reflect that change. This booklet is simply a medium – like a mulch to clear the weeds – helping to guide allotment gardening into the 21st century. I hope it is useful to you while you need it. Afterwards, pass it on to a friend or compost it.

history

This section is a potted history of land ownership in Britain and the development of allotments for cultivation by people without access to land. It is important at this point to stress that land ownership – even up to the present day – is and has been simply a series of rights over land. Modern landowners still share the rights to their land with the state. They are required to apply for planning permission to change land use, and to respect the existence of public footpaths, for example. The history of land use in this country can be seen in the development of rights to the land, and how those rights have changed up to the present day.

In Saxon times land was owned by peasant farmers – ceorls – who held smallholdings and also farmed some land communally. Food, rent and military service were exacted from these peasants by the king. The Norman conquest abolished land ownership by the peasant farmers and imposed a complex hierarchical feudal system in its place. This new structure placed God at the top, through whom the King was divinely empowered. Beneath the King, Britain was now split between 180 Barons, expected to keep a paternalistic eye on those beneath them. Under William the Conqueror 'nobody could till the soil unless he paid for it, whether by providing free labour or military service.' (This Land Is Our Land, p18) However, common rights to land - particularly gathering fuel and food and grazing on 'waste' land in the manor, was an ancient British right, and left untouched by Norman feudalism, in part, because changing it was more trouble than it was worth.

From the 12th century onwards, common land began to be enclosed by noblemen keen to demonstrate their wealth and power. They created deer parks and large gardens and made money from timber, sheep pasture, and large-scale agriculture. Gradually, a series of local

Inclosure Acts swept away the commons and changed agricultural work patterns. People found themselves dispossessed of the land from which they had previously scraped a subsistence. This dispossession resulted in much spare labour which eventually migrated to the cities and the new factories that sprang up during the Industrial Revolution. It also resulted in death from starvation for many of the new landless.

There was protest about the enclosures. In 1649 Gerrard Winstanley and the Diggers set up a colony on St George's Hill in Surrey as a direct action against the enclosures which were making tilling common land illegal. The local landowner, with the support of the army, drove the Diggers out – but not before their crops were destroyed, and their rough houses burnt to the ground. The Diggers could be described as the first socialists. With no earlier political thought to go by, Winstanley used a lot of biblical imagery to expain his beliefs on equality. He died a Quaker, a new religion at that time - which gives some idea of where he was coming from.

Protest continued, however. The Riot Act of 1715 was created specifically for the Inclosure Acts. And this was war. The new, enclosing, landowner was empowered to read the Riot Act to any protestors, and at the end to 'cut down' any remaining protestors. The Riot Act was followed by the Black Acts of 1723 which created 50 new capital offences against the anti-enclosure riots. How much difference this made to a dispossessed population threatened with starvation is anyone's guess.

By the early 19th century, much of Britain was urbanised and many people no longer made their living from the land. However, workers often supplemented their meagre incomes by working strips of common land. In places where land was not available, the Poor Laws ensured that churchwardens and overseers of the poor were empowered to provide allotment land 'by way of making able-bodied paupers work for their keep' (*Law of Allotments, p4*). The rules of these new allotments often included church going and sobriety rules in an attempt at social control.

The General Inclosure Act of 1845 saw the completion of the process of enclosure. This act unlike previous Inclosure Acts made rudimentary allotment provision for the 'labouring poor' mandatory. The size and extent of such land was not specified and, as such, was often not sufficiently provided. Subsequent legislation tightened up this obligation, but again it was easy to wriggle out of it. Landowners often made taking an allotment impossible, by charging ridiculous rents, or providing unworkable or distant land.

Allotment provision was not always popular with employers or landowners. Although their contributions to subsistence kept wages and Poor Relief low, this had its flip side. In the words of a contemporary writer, it was felt that 'the holding of an allotment will give the labourer a spirit of independence that will interfere with the service he owes his master.' (*The Allotment, p54*).

Although land was provided on which to grow food, the legislation surrounding it made it clear that the rules were those of landlord and tenant – it was not common land. In many ways this protected allotments from abuse, but it also meant that rules and regulations of tenancy imposed the conditions of servitude upon allotment holders. An 1843 Government Report on allotments stated that allotment provision 'should not become an inducement to neglect his usual paid labour, [and therefore] the allotment should be of no greater extent that can be cultivated during the leisure moments of the family.' (*The Allotment, p.49*).

The 1845 General Inclosure Act provoked protest from local co-operative groups who could not survive adequately without their own cultivatable land, and also protest from urban dwellers who wanted some countryside for recreation. The allotments movement had begun in earnest – and it was this struggle over land which, again, can be seen as one of the roots of the socialist movement in Britain.

In 1884, the vote was extended to the male agricultural labourer and this brought the allotments issue to Parliament. In 1886, the issue of land, inclosure and allotments brought down Lord Salisbury's (Conservative) government. When the Conservative government was later reinstated, they rushed through the Allotment Act of 1887, which, followed by the Act of 1890, made allotment provision for the 'labouring poor' compulsory.

The 1908 Allotments Act finally made allotments provision the responsibility of local authorities, and the 1922 Allotments Act made allotments available to all, not only the labouring poor 'where a need was shown to exist'. The first and second world wars saw a huge increase in allotment provision. By World War II, there were one and a half million plots, as opposed to 300,000 now. Vegetable cultivation was promoted as part of Britain's war-time self-sufficiency drive. In fact, up until the 1950s, allotments were seen as part of Britain's Civil Defence. As the threat of war dissolved, society changed. Apart from a brief post-war Dig for Plenty campaign, allotment vegetable cultivation was no longer encouraged – people's labour and also leisure time was more valuable spent elsewhere in the economy.

In 1964 the then Labour Government commissioned Harry Thorpe's Committe of Inquiry into Allotments, which produced its report in 1969. Looking at what allotments had become in the post-war years, one of its main suggestions was that they should be renamed 'leisure gardens' as gardening was seen as an increasingly recreational activity. People who used them did so because they wanted to, not because urban agriculture was crucial to life.

The Thorpe Committee Report on allotments identified a new breed of allotment gardener. Far from being the active political being of the Victorian era, Thorpe saw the modern allotmenteer as 'primarily an individualist who considers his allotment to be as private as his home garden, who is seldom interested in anything beyond its boundaries, and is blind to his further responsibilities' (quoted in *The Allotment, p117*). It is this individualism – provoked by an increased post-war alienation and the 'I'm all right Jack' consumer culture which has played into the hands of developers. The allotments movement has forgotten its community roots, and the origins of allotments as a replacement for common land.

The Thorpe Report was not acted upon by government – again, allotments were not seen as crucial to a healthy economy or society. They weren't an urgent issue and so they were sidelined. Since the Act in 1950 through to the latter half of the 20th century allotment law had been increasingly eroded, and allotments have ended up in a cul-de-sac of their own. No longer linked to agriculture, or to community, it has become difficult to place them within the industrial world of the modern vegetable consumer.

legislation

Within the law of contract, allotments law is a specialised branch of Landlord and Tenant, and a branch which is the product of statute. Unfortunately, the relevant statutes are many and of considerable age; the recommendations of the Thorpe Committee that "all existing allotments legislation should be repealed and replaced by a single new Act", has not yet been implemented.
J. F. Garner, The Law of Allotments, 1984.

The Thorpe Committee's report came out over 30 years ago, and allotments legislation was seen as confusing and outdated then. To give you some idea of the minefield we are in now, over half a century after the last allotment law was enacted, it is useful to have some idea of the legal state of play, but also very easy to get caught up in the twists and turns of the outdated law. Much argument on interpretation is enjoyed by allotment law specialists – it is so vague. If you're into being a legal eagle, train-spotting for minor points and repeals and later amendments, then allotment law is for you. Personally, it drives me nuts.

It is also worth bearing in mind that due to the gradual erosion, repeals and amendments of allotments legislation since the last Allotment Act in 1950, you are unlikely to get any useful information from reading any of the allotment laws in their original formats. A very good way of checking some of this out is to look at the JUSTIS CD-ROM, available in all main libraries. It shows you which laws are applicable to the area you are searching in, which sections have been repealed or amended, and which laws they have been repealed into. It does make you dizzy after an hour or so, but it is worth it.

Alternatively, for technophobes, legal libraries and good reference libraries have current volumes of Halsbury's Statutes, which covers all the latest legal state of play. The Chronological Table of Statutes is a shorter, cheaper, two-volume set which offers much the same thing and should be more widely available. Both are published by The Stationery Office (www.hmso.gov.uk), who also supply individual Acts and Statutes. However, an extra brownie point for the JUSTIS CD-ROM is that some versions also have case law on them – particularly useful if you are in the middle of a legal case. Case law is also available free from the Bailii website, (www.bailii.org). I think a lawyer is always recommended for actual legal battles, although people do fight their own cases. There is free legal advice available if you choose this route (more on this later).

Relevant allotments legislation

Below are outlined the basic laws with some of their main points which still stand, or which show how those laws have been eroded (actual wording from the legislation is in italics). These will be useful in your campaigning or daily allotment business. You may find that in the course of rummaging through legislation and case law you unearth some new, relevant legal gem I have overlooked which will be of real help in your case. Try to spread the word about this (through contacts network at the back) so it can be useful to other cases elsewhere. I have included only legislation applying to England and Wales. Scotland has its own similar legislation, enacted in conjunction with relevant English/Welsh laws.

The Small Holdings and Allotments Act, 1908
- replaced the earlier allotment laws
- outlined the local authority's duty to provide allotments to the labouring population
- Section 23 of the Act states that the local authority has a duty to provide *a sufficient number of allotments if they are of the opinion* that there is a demand for them
- Section 23 also states that if six ratepayers of an area, where there was no existing allotment provision, wrote to the local authority asking for an allotment, then that authority would be obliged to *take proceedings* for allotment provision, *and the council shall take such representation into consideration.* (The exception to this are the 12 boroughs of Inner London, which are no longer obliged to provide allotments. This requirement was removed by Section 55(4) of the London Government Act of 1963)

- Section 32(1) permits local authorities to sell land *if they are of the opinion* that the land is not needed for the purposes of allotments
- Section 32(2) requires any profits made by local authorities from the sale of allotment land to be used to pay any debts associated with allotment land, or to acquire, adapt, or improve other land for allotments. Any surplus can be used by the local authority for general funds
- Section 25(2) gives the local authority power to compulsorily purchase land for allotments if land cannot be provided by private agreement. The Secretary of State is the confirming authority of compulsory purchase orders (CPOs)
- Section 26 says that local authorities may make improvements to allotment land – drainage, paths, sheds, etc.
- Section 27 (5) allows a council to lease allotment land for commercial use as long as it returns to allotment cultivation if required.

The Allotments Act, 1922

- provided some security of tenure and improved compensation for terminating tenancies
- Section 1 requires 12 months' notice to quit for an allotment garden. The notice must expire on or before 6 April or on or after 29 September in any year
- Section 22.1 updated the definition of an 'allotment garden' as *not exceeding 40 poles* (1000 square metres/quarter of an acre) *in extent which is wholly or mainly cultivated by the occupier for the production of vegetables and fruit crops for consumption by himself and his family*. This has remained the definition to this day.

The Allotments Act, 1925

- Section 8 also states that statutory sites cannot be disposed of (sold or converted to other purposes) without ministerial consent. The Secretary of State must be satisfied that adequate provision will be made *for allotment holders displaced by the action of the local authority or that such provision is unnecessary or not reasonably practicable.*

Town and Country Planning Act, 1947

- repealed Section 3 of the Allotments Act, 1925. This meant that local authorities no longer had to consider reserving land for allotments provision in their local plans.

The Allotments Act, 1950

- further improved security of tenure and compensation for termination of tenancy
- increased expenditure on allotments expected by local authorities
- modified the 1908 Act on provision by saying that local councils have a statutory obligation to provide *allotment gardens* only, in populations exceeding 10,000 people
- the size of each statutory plot was limited to no more than 20 poles (500 square meters/an eighth of an acre) in extent
- allowed tenants to keep certain forms of livestock on allotment gardens – particularly rabbits and chickens
- Section 10 requires that an allotment must be let at a rent which *a tenant may reasonably be expected to pay for the land.* This rent may be lowered under special circumstances (to those on low incomes - the unemployed or pensioners, for example).

1972 Local Government Act

- removed the obligation for local authorities to appoint allotment committees as set out in Section 12 of the 1925 Act.

1980 Local Government Planning and Land Act

- the Department of the Environment was no longer obliged to collect local authority statistics on allotment gardening and on waiting lists, which therefore also applied to local authorities
- Section 28 of the 1908 Act amended – the alteration of rules and conditions of cultivation no longer require the approval of the Secretary of State. Certain baseline rules still apply, defined by local conditions and what is contained in allotment laws
- the requirement that local authorities keep separate allotment accounts and that revenue receipts in such accounts should only be used for allotment purposes was repealed.

Legal eagles may be interested in checking other acts relating to allotment law:

- *1971 Town and Country Planning Act*
- *1981 Acquisition of Land Act*
- *1919 Land Settlement (Facilities) Act*
- *1926 Smallholdings and Allotments Act*

Some of these laws have substantial parts that are not relevant, or have been repealed, but there still may be something there of interest. The JUSTIS CD-ROM may point you in their direction anyway. At the moment, there is unlikely to be any change in allotment law, and it is both up to precedent and us within the allotments movement to change the way things are done.

Categories of allotment site

Statutory sites

These sites make up the bulk of allotment sites (74%). Owned by the local authority, and entirely governed by allotments legislation, they have legal protection and cannot be sold unless it can be demonstrated to the Secretary of State that a site is no longer needed for allotments, and would be better used for alternative development. The Secretary of State, working through the Office of the Deputy Prime Minister (ODPM), tends to trust local council reports on dereliction and the reasons for it, and agrees on sales based on their reports.

Temporary sites

Rented by the local authority from a private owner for the purposes of allotments or owned by the local authority but destined for some other use. This type of allotment site has also recently become popular with local councils. They make up 13% of allotment provision. There are no statutory protections for tenants on temporary allotments under the allotment acts. However, prospective developers need planning permission first before building, and this can be denied, which also applies to private sites.

Private sites

These are neither owned nor leased by local authorities. Therefore they are not governed by any of the allotments legislation. They cover about 8% of all allotment land (statistics from the David Crouch/NSALG Allotments Survey 1997). It is also worth bearing in mind that there is no national standard of allotment provision. Although councils have to provide allotments, the number of allotments per head is not defined, and left up to the individual authorities.

Additional legislation

You could look at the complex legal minefield surrounding allotments and simply want to give up. Don't − there's more, and it's much more fun, up-to-date, easy to understand, and interesting than the legal system. Some of it also gives us the possibility of widening the uses for allotments. Local councils often have to make up ways of dealing with allotments as they go along. You can often use this to your advantage and forward-thinking local councils may ignore legislation in favour of expediency. New directives from central government can force councils to push aside outdated and confused legislation.

These policy areas include Planning Policy Guidance Notes (see Chapter 6, *Protection*), which are legally binding – useful for allotments under threat, and Local Agenda 21 (see Chapter 5, *Reinvention*) – useful for all aspects of allotment use, from best practice to legal protection. LA21 is particularly important here because it can set allotments in a modern framework – it includes environment and community.

Local authority Best Value Plans

Although councils no longer have to appoint allotment committees, there are other ways to check that a local authority is doing its job. All councils should have a Best Value Plan; a new national initiative that must have been in place by April 2000. A key part of the Best Value Plan includes community consultation, of all services, including tendered ones. However, before private companies are considered, they must have proper policies, including equal opportunities and environmental codes. This is particularly useful for allotments as councils often take responsibility for infrastructural work on sites and you should have a say in this, as well as their management overall.

Core Values

Linked to Best Value Plans are Core Values which all councils should already have, highlighting their central beliefs. As with much policy, this often looks good but isn't always reflected in action. It can be used as a gentle reminder for councils going awry – a prod in the right direction. (For more campaigning tactics, see Chapter 7, *Campaign*.)

The Select Committee Report: The Future for Allotments, 1998

This is an important document. Although its recommendations did not become law, it carries weight because it was produced by an 'all-party' committee of MPs. It is very much on the side of allotment holders and sees allotments as a valuable resource that needs protecting. It recommended urgent action by the government to protect existing allotment sites. Although the government took very little notice of its recommendations, it can still be useful in adding bite to any campaign. The report drew up 29 conclusions and recommendations.

Key recommendations were:
- Allotments legislation should be overhauled. New legislation should be put in place incorporating all the 29 recommendations.
- Temporary sites in use for over thirty years should become statutory (unless marked for cemeteries).
- The owners of private sites should 'where appropriate, adopt a long-term and positive approach' towards their allotments.
- Sale of statutory sites should involve plot-holder consultation.
- Waiting lists and applications for statutory plots should be publicly accessible.
- Before selling a site, the local authority should have an Allotment Officer; provide water and fencing; be promoting allotment use; and have put notice boards on all sites with contact/letting details.
- Decent, local, statutory replacement sites should be found for sites sold, or significant reinvestment should take place in existing sites.
- Restrictions on cultivation, particularly flower growing, keeping of livestock, selling surplus produce and site shops, should be repealed.
- Local authorities should look into and promote self-management of their sites.

The Government's response

The 1998 Government Select Committee took six months to come up with its recommendations, but, rather than overhauling all the legislation and really changing the situation, the Government failed to act, and where it did was rather weak. Its overall attitude was expressed in the immortal comment: "It should be recognised that allotment gardening already enjoys far greater legal protection than other worthwhile leisure activities."

The Select Committee did make two policy recommendations, however. The first was that before a council sold off a site, it should be able to show that it had effectively promoted it (more on this in Chapter 6, *Protection*). It also suggested that the Local Government Association produce a set of best practice guidelines on allotment use for local authorities.

Best Practice Guidelines for Local Authorities

Published in 2001, these guidelines are aimed primarily at council allotment managers to help them develop better allotment strategies. They draw on the experience of about twenty local authorities with a history of good practice on allotments and cover planning and legislation as well as being strong on sustainability.

The guide is useful for activists as it presents the point of view of government and Local Authorities and ties in with new thinking on the subject. Although in itself it won't change the original legal structure, as a policy document it will build upon the slow process of change. It also includes much valuable information, tips and pointers.

Government Policy Papers

It is useful to keep your eyes peeled for related government policy which affects allotment use. This will be particularly in the fields of planning (see Chapter 6, *Protection*), sustainability (see Chapter 5, *Reinvention*), and urban open space. The Office of the Deputy Prime Minister (ODPM) is now the government department responsible for allotments (it is also responsible for housing, planning, devolution, regional and local government, and the fire service).

Government policy is only as current as the government issuing it, but the ideas it contains do tend to filter down and have an effect. Wheels set in motion by governments usually continue for some time afterwards. European legislation is also relevant, as it covers community and environmental legislation. It will be increasingly useful for the protection of green space in the UK.

Urban White Paper

The first Urban White Paper for 20 years, called *Our Towns and Cities: The Future - Delivering an Urban Renaissance*, came out in November 2000. It focuses on regeneration issues and makes a clear commitment to maintaining and improving the quality of urban open space. It offers a clear commitment from Government on sustainability and community involvement in planning, recognising that social, economic, and environmental issues are interdependent.

Urban Green Spaces – Report and Policy

The Government created the Urban Green Spaces Task Force in 2001 to advise on improving the quality of urban parks, play areas and green spaces. Its report, Green Spaces, Better Places was produced in May 2002. This states that urban spaces contribute to the sustainability of towns and cities, and to a better quality of life. Amongst other things, it states that planners and planning should take more account of urban open space.

The Government's urban green spaces policy statement was published in October 2002 as part of the public space report *Living Places - Cleaner, Safer, Greener*. It states: 'The Government is committed to the creation of networks of accessible, good quality parks and diverse green spaces in all our towns and cities'. It sets out proposals for providing stronger leadership and more focus on green spaces. It also responds to the Task Force report, outlining plans which include better local strategic planning, encouraging more community engagement, and better use of resources. Additionally, it committed to improving the quality of the green space information base, which includes updating the 1997 English Allotments Survey. At the time of writing, the new Allotment Survey is due out in mid-2005, from the University of Derby, or the ODPM.

Linking into relevant campaigns and organisations will keep you informed of developments through newsletters and other information (see *Contacts List*). It is up to us in the allotments movement to continue the process of change by action and resourcefulness more than by recourse to legal structures. Through our successful activities and high-profile campaigning, we can bring allotments and green open space use onto the national agenda.

Organisation

Self-management at some level by allotment holders for allotment holders is the cornerstone of all successful allotment sites and projects. In a perfect world maybe you could rely on your council to do it all for you. However, allotments are not as urgent an issue for councils as education or housing. This means that cash-strapped councils do not always have spare funds to manage their sites effectively.

Bristol City Council Allotment Manager, Steve Clampin, says: "We take in £80,000 in rents, but our water bills alone come to £45,000, before maintenance, repairs, and skip hire which tenants want. There is a lot of pressure on us to dispose of sites even with high turnovers." This is one reason to support allotment self-management – taking the responsibility and the need for funding out of council's hands. "Using volunteers reduces costs," says Clampin, "and groups can often get funding where councils can't. It's up to the Allotment Office to support and facilitate it."

The most successful sites tend to combine a strong, well-organised allotment association working alongside a supportive council with a commitment to environmental policy, and the resources to provide an adequate infrastructure. But at the end of the day, you and your neighbours use the allotments, understand the site and what it and the community around it needs. It's your land, you use it – why not manage it as well?

There are many ways to bring about an effective group. The first stage is always to start talking to people on the site to get a sense of what people are feeling. It is important that you don't work alone. Recruit allies, then inform everyone working on and living around your site that you are getting a group together or revitalise the old one. Your initial plan should simply be to form a strong association around the allotment site, unless the allotment is urgently under threat. Later on you and your group will want to work together to address specific issues which you all agree are important.

Be sure to involve original members of the association – try to recruit a team to join in planning the meeting. Get a list of everyone on your site from your landlord if you can, and make use of (or create) a site noticeboard. Make brightly coloured, simple and easy-to-read posters and leaflets to attract as many people to the new group as possible. Ask for feedback and advice to shape the meeting's agenda, make the group as open and inclusive as possible, and include contact details. Your site will contain all sorts of people with many valuable skills, talents, and experience. If you can engage this pool of resources you can create a vibrant team in no time.

Hold a meeting

Bear in mind that the purpose of the first meeting is to get a group together and find out any issues that need to be addressed. A good idea to begin with is to hold a meeting possibly with a social, to relax people and build unity (if your social includes a drink, it's best to have it afterwards). Try to choose a neutral venue if you can – it's OK to charge a pound or two to those attending for the hire of a community or church hall. Contact your local community association – they may even provide the venue free to community groups, or for your first meeting, particularly if they have a stake in the new association.

The way meetings are run can make or break organisations. There's nothing worse than long rambling meetings which decide nothing, or for one person to hijack the meeting and drone on endlessly about their favourite hobbyhorse. This is a guaranteed method for putting people off. Make your meetings clear, concise and short. It's better to have more short meetings than fewer long meetings.

How to run a meeting

The most common method is to have a Chair who keeps the meeting running smoothly and introduces the topics, together with a Secretary who keeps notes of the meeting and notes any points of action. Sometimes meetings can be daunting to those not used to them. Quieter members often need encouragement to express their views so they don't feel ignored and withdraw from the process.

Some examples of effective techniques can be found below in *General Tips* and check Contacts List and Bibliography for more information and advice.

Your meeting will need to be clear about its purpose and its time guidelines. Make sure your agenda is clear and simple, and try to circulate or display it beforehand. This first meeting should decide future group aims and objectives. These will include how you want to form, and/or the issues you all want to tackle. You may decide you want to concentrate on projects or events, or filling all plots, and leave financial site administration to the council for example. You may choose to make decisions by consensus or 'nearly consensus' rather than simple majority. Consensus decision-making often takes longer, but can be very positive for group inclusivity and unity (check *Seeds for Change* for more details).

If you have no experience of facilitating meetings, most councils should have a Community Development department which should be able to help you. Alternatively, your local volunteer bureau or environment centre may be able to point you in the right direction or help set up and run your first meeting. Don't be afraid to ask for help from other groups you trust; setting up and running meetings is a skill you can acquire like any other.

General tips:

- Agree ground rules before the meeting begins - no swearing, no aggressive behaviour, everyone listening to everyone else etc.
- Get everyone present at the meeting to introduce themselves before the meeting starts and say what they want the meeting/association to achieve. If similar ideas come up at this stage, you may want to amend the agenda accordingly.
- Appoint a level-headed Chair or facilitator. They don't have to know everything about allotments - they're just there to ensure the meeting runs well. They could be external (a well respected member of the community, for example). They should be firm enough to stop strong personalities dominating the meeting, and sensitive enough to encourage shy people.
- If a related, but not central issue comes up which needs discussion - try to create a sub-group and/or set up another meeting to discuss it later.
- Elect people to take responsibilities for the areas you consider important, and decide how much decision-making authority the group wants them to have. If you decide to adopt a constitution (which you will certainly need if you are to apply for funding) you will need people to assume various roles; these will include Chair, Secretary, and Treasurer. You may want to add Events Organiser, Lettings Secretary, or Tree Surgeon - whatever takes your fancy!
- Decide how often to have meetings - meetings are boring for many people. Separate projects or an appointed 'steering group' may want to meet more often, or you may want to stick to the traditional AGM and Committee structure (see *Constitutions*, below).
- Try and deal with major decisions or thorny issues earlier in the meeting when people are fresher and more alert. Alternatively set the agenda at the beginning of each meeting based on current issues and get those present to prioritise the order things are discussed.
- Ask people to speak in the first person - 'I' think this should happen rather than 'they' should do something or other.
- The use of the 'go round', when each person present is given a short time to speak to the whole group without interruptions - especially useful at the point in the meeting just before a decision is to be taken.
- Don't be afraid to call a break in the meeting to let people stretch their legs or cool down after a heated discussion.

- Make sure everyone can see or knows the major decisions taken and accepts and/or understands them before the end of the meeting.
- Take note of agreed action points and review progress at the next meeting.
- Take a list of the names and contact details for all those present and send minutes (however brief) or agreed action points of decisions taken and a reminder of the next meeting.
- Have a clear end time and stick to it. Try to rein people in from going off too much on tangents.
- Remember not to finish the meeting without setting a date or a venue for the next one.

Don't let your meeting become a place where people moan about what's wrong – time is short, and you could lose useful people that way. Try to locate what needs to be done to address the issues and then work towards it.

As a group, try to be as open and accountable as possible. If people aren't active members they are just as valuable and need to be kept informed of developments. You don't need to post updates to everyone, but have agreed places – noticeboard, community association etc, where minutes and other information are posted.

Constitutions

If your group is to have anything to do with money, you will need a bank account, unless one of you can be trusted to keep your funds in a petty cash box under the shed. One of the requirements of an organisation having a bank account is a constitution. If you decide to collect rents you will also need a bank account, and you will need to lease your site from the council. For this, you will also need a constitution. I was Secretary of a site in Oxford which didn't have a bank account, but needed to apply for a grant and couldn't locate their old constitution – this gave us a chance to discuss the issues involved and decide upon a new one.

Constitutions vary depending upon what kind of association you want to form. They could be companies or trusts, but allotment associations, which are not trading or dealing with enormous assets, tend to form as Unincorporated Associations. You don't really need to know what this means except that it's the least hassle of all constituted bodies, and the most open. Legally, Unincorporated Associations must have in their constitution:

- **name** of the Association
- **objectives** of the Association
- **membership** with voting entitlement
- an **Annual General Meeting** (AGM) which elects major posts and the Committee, and decides on policy
- a **Chair** (calls and facilitates meetings, although rotating facilitation is also useful)
- a **Secretary** (deals with day-to-day running of group)
- a **Treasurer** (does accounts and deals with cash)
- how many people make up a **quorum**. This is the number of people required to make valid policy decisions.

A model allotment association constitution is attached in the appendices. Outline descriptions of the roles of an allotment Secretary, Treasurer, and Chair and other help with constitutions can be obtained from your local volunteer bureau or Allotments Federation, the Scottish Allotments and Gardens Society or The National Society of Allotment and Leisure Gardeners (NSALG), (amongst others!). You can modify anything you need to, as long as you have named people in the main posts, a voting membership, and an AGM. A set of agreed rules can be useful even for unconstituted bodies – revised by the group annually or as needed.

(It's also worth remembering that however important a constitution is, don't lose sleep over it. Constitutions are simply useful legal documents which often end up in a file drawer never to be looked at, whilst the group itself is out changing the world.)

Lease – working with the Council Allotments Office

Depending upon how much responsibility you want to take for self-management, you may need to sign a lease between yourselves and your local authority. Bristol City Council offers two different types of lease, depending upon how much responsibility the allotment association wants to take for their site. Remember, it's entirely up to you – if you don't like the lease, don't sign it, or see if you can begin a process to get it modified.

The Sturminster Road Allotment Association in Bristol formed a project called Spadeworks in 1992 to regenerate the site. They have regenerated the 30-plot site to almost full occupancy, and have created a wildlife garden. Spadeworks helps with the day to day running of the site, clearing plots, advertising the site, and receiving grants for equipment without having an allotments lease. At the end of the day, the Council deals with the rent money, and the applications, but Spadeworks keep things running very smoothly. Jean Mantle, Secretary of Spadeworks says: "We've always recruited our own plot-holders, we've never had anyone referred directly from the Council. We all work together - you need a committee, but we work together and help each other."

Sympathetic Allotment Officers are wonderful allies and support for advice, information, and practical help. Sound them out - they won't necessarily bite you. A flourishing allotment site is a string to their bow – it shows they're doing their job well. It also depends upon how you approach them, particularly as many people view councils negatively, and this often makes council employees wary and easily defensive. Be positive and direct. And whatever the outcome, if your association is united, do it your way. Often councils have allotments panels or committees made up of representatives from sites and associations. These are a good way to get your views heard and network with other sites and associations in your area. Shelagh Wilson, from the Hasting Federation says: 'Be clear on what you want, and do point sheets to send in advance to every meeting to influence agendas.'

Networking
National and local networks are very useful for allotment associations to get a wider sense of the issues involved, and support and advice when they need it. For 70 years, allotment associations and plot-holders have been officially networked and represented by the National Society for Allotment and Leisure Gardeners (NSALG). Their structure works similarly to political parties, pressure groups with local offices, and the Trades Union Movement. Local associations send representatives to the regional Federation of Allotment and Leisure Gardeners, which in turn send representatives to vote and stand for office at the Annual General Meeting (AGM) of the National Society of Allotment and Leisure

Gardeners. The NSALG deals with national allotment issues, provides legal and practical advice, and sends allotment associations a quarterly newsletter to keep them up to date.

Sadly the NSALG has lost members over the past decade. The slack has often been taken up by various community groups and non-federated allotment associations. However, the NSALG still has many thousands of members and are supportive of community groups and projects like those outlined in this book. They also are keen to bring about change in UK allotment law and are worth trying if you have a thorny problem.

If you are already working from within a strong and representative Federation, of which there are many, or you can tap into this network for support and expertise, then stick with it. As mentioned earlier some Federations are not joined to the National, but have formed independently as local networks. You may find you are from an area which does not have a strong Federation, but it may be useful to join the National Society anyway, just to keep up to date with many of the issues and get advice on practical allotment legalities. Whatever your situation, liaising with other local allotment sites and associations is very useful. You can swap tips and best practice ideas. It also gives you a united front if you find you are experiencing any difficulties with the council etc.

Do try to ensure you have an external support network, especially at local level. You might find it very useful to ally yourself with a local community association, horticultural group, or other bodies who can advise and support you as you go.

Understanding differences

It's true to say that wherever you get human interaction, along with the good things like cooperation, there will also be disagreement. Allotments in particular can be hotbeds for argument, because they represent a dwindling community resource. Land, and how it is used, is a perennial area of conflict.

Strong organizations need to allow for conflict and argument – it shapes them and keeps them on their toes. Good management also keeps things in perspective; differences can easily be forgotten when there's a common and imperative aim to focus upon (like the cohesive spirit of wartime or other crisis situations).

Sometimes cultural or ideological differences, or personality clashes can become barriers and cause for argument, rather than opportunities to grow and change. Association ground rules can be very important here (see Bullying, below). Don't ignore problems and hope that they will go away. Talk out and understand differences rather than be split by them. Regardless of who they are, everyone needs to feel supported, listened to, and equal. Improve your internal communication skills. Councils, and voluntary and community associations can often also help with good management skills, equalities training, and mediation.

If things cannot be handled satisfactorily within the group, mediation is a way of helping to resolve problems and come up with an agreement everyone accepts. It relies upon a trained, neutral, third party mediator (check the Contacts List for details of services.) Alternatively, if you are linked to a larger body, like your Allotments Federation, or a community group, you can use this as a forum to sort things out. You often just need someone, or an organisation you all trust, to separate the wood from the trees. Then you can all get back on track to start tackling the serious issues.

Problems can't always be resolved and consensus can't always be reached, especially if the group doesn't share common goals and commitments. If you've all had a good go at dealing with the issue, and haven't still haven't agreed; if the same issues continue to arise over which you cannot compromise, you may choose to leave the group. Find another group, or go it alone elsewhere. However, don't burn your bridges. You may not be able to be part of this group, but at the end of the day you are all from the same community, and may need to work together in the future.

Bullying

For any group or allotment site to work smoothly, whatever internal wrangles it has, it is essential that all members treat others with respect and dignity. Everyone gets heated from time to time, but when the site contains people who thrive on victimisation and negativity, it is essential you take action.

The recommended website www.bullyonline.org describes bullying as '…persistent unwelcome behaviour, [including] …unwarranted or invalid criticism, nit-picking, fault-finding …exclusion, isolation, being singled out and treated differently, being shouted at, humiliated, excessive monitoring, [and] having verbal and written warnings imposed…'

There are different reasons for bullying and different types of bully, although it is always caused by inadequacy and fear. Usually it is sweet, harmless people who are bullied, and bullies look for any vulnerability in people to use against them. Some people are more vulnerable than others – women and minority groups – or anybody obviously different from the group 'norm'.

Bullying can be caused by temporary stress. People often take allotments to 'get away from it all' and it can be very difficult when suddenly a new group of strange looking people descend upon them. They might feel threatened by anyone who turns up and challenges their comfortable world view, is unfamiliar, or does things differently, (including organic and/or permaculture methods). Sometimes, however, groups develop dysfunctional cultures and contain very unpleasant people who thrive on power games and conflict (serial bullies). Serial bullies can be very charming and manipulative, whilst in private victimising their targets to within an inch of their lives.

Whatever the reason you are being bullied, it is not acceptable, and you must challenge it. Go to your allotments association, or council allotments officer, and ask them what their strategy is for dealing with problems on allotments. If you do not feel confident doing this on your own, recruit an ally to help you. Adopt a clause in your constitution that sets out an equal opportunities policy giving everyone equal status regardless of age, disability, race, gender, sexuality, or culture (all councils, and most businesses and organisations have them). The Borough of Reigate and Banstead asks all allotment holders to sign a 'Dignity Statement' (see Appendices), which commits plot-holders to equalities and good behaviour – they face losing their plots if they don't comply.

If the bully is a reasonable person, problems can usually be sorted out with mediation or discussion. It is important that both sides listen to how the other feels, and understanding can be reached. For obvious reasons, mediation doesn't work with serial bullies.

Bullies often disappear into the woodwork once they are challenged, or you can show you are strong. Don't back down. Tell the bully that you will not accept their behaviour. Remain calm and detached from any negativity – do not enter into argument with irrational people - you won't win. It is difficult to feel strong if you are isolated. Gather a strong, supportive group around you. If you are working your plot alone, take a mate or two down to help (and to provide witnesses if necessary).

Caroline Fernandez, of the Women's Environmental Network, says: 'There were problems with harassment of women on one of the projects in the network, they sorted it out by talking to the men who were doing the harassment, and organising days when the women went down in groups, which made them feel more confident.'

In some situations, if you cannot find justice, and the problem continues, walking away is the best thing to do. Bullying and harassment cause people psychological injury, and it is impossible to function properly under these conditions. It is important you regain control of the situation. Choose to move on and find a site which values you and your skills. Write to your allotments officer and tell them why you have left the site.

Where appropriate, talk about the bullying. 'Shame, embarrassment, guilt, and fear are encouraged by the bully,' says bullyonline.org, 'for this is how all abusers control and silence their victims.' Whatever happens, don't be silenced, and don't blame yourself.

So there you have it; group working – the good, the bad, and the downright nasty. Lets stick to the good and look at ways you can work together to turn your site around.

promotion

So, you've formed or are rejuvenating your allotment association. Right now, if there aren't any other pressing issues to be dealt with (like a threatened site), you will probably want to look at how to attract and keep allotment holders. And if your site's in a state, you're not in the best PR position in the world.

Ending 'The Cycle of Dereliction'

The Cycle of Dereliction is a well-documented problem. Disused allotment sites can attract vandalism, so they lose plot holders and fail to attract new gardeners, which attracts more vandalism, and the cycle goes on...

Many sites are in danger because they are not filled – they are seen as derelict by councils and the Secretary of State can therefore authorise selling them off. Also, some councils will not let plots on sites they are planning to sell, which highlights the importance of good self-management. Even names on council waiting lists can be enough to delay sell off due to vacancy.

It is possible to turn around a derelict site in a relatively short time. Below are some tips to help you with this.

Security

Security is a very important factor. If your site's not safe, new allotment holders may experience problems and be put off. Invest in fences and gates, give everyone keys, and try to make sure everyone locks up after themselves. This can be expensive (see Chapter 5, *Reinvention*, for fundraising information).

A cheap and cheerful way of deterring vandals is to grow impenetrable blackthorn or any of the wild roses, which are very pretty, (*Rosa rugosa* contains large edible rosehips too), or other thick and thorny plants, although this can take longer. (Here, however, the gardener's nightmare – the bramble – could prove to be a great ally. Keep 'em clipped back, and they'll make an effective, edible fence/hedge).

Many allotment associations which experience continuing problems with intruders cultivate good relationships with their local police, who can be of help not just with policing, but also with grants and advice. Some associations form their own 'Allotment Watch' to keep an eye out for intruders.

Vandalism

Vandalism is a very unpleasant way of discovering just how some sections of the local community feel towards their allotments. Crucially, the land is not seen as theirs – people do not usually destroy something in which they have a stake. Obviously, security is important, but just as important is an inclusive feeling. Open events and projects can encourage local people to feel protective towards the site and its tenants, rather than destructive. This has been shown with work in prison and community gardens in the US. Responsibility for the shape of the land can be empowering and provide a sense of self, pride, and achievement.

Even one or two protective people can do a lot to discourage vandalism in others. Cultivate good relationships with your neighbours – this can also be very useful for security, particularly if their houses overlook the site. Maybe put a plot aside for community use, and ask local people what they want. This won't always be to grow vegetables in the first instance. Don't worry – see if you can adapt to provide what they need - it's better than getting your crops trashed. (It could be a barbecue area for the grown-ups or even a BMX cycle track for the local kids; maybe you could adapt some of the paths!) Whatever it is will be a start, and once they're on the site, feeling good about it – all kinds of other ideas and growing ideas often follow.

Contact youth and community workers and groups for event and project ideas, input and advice. They might well be supportive of an important, inclusive community project, particularly if it involves the chance to do much-needed fund raising. (See Chapter 5, *Reinvention*.)

Clear your site

Overgrown plots are more difficult to let than plots which are ready for planting. For this, you will need labour and equipment to get the worst bits cleared, covered with a plastic or carpet mulch, ready for the next allotment holder. Alternatively, if you think the plot may be out of use for a while, you could turn it to grass - then you just need to keep the grass cut, which should be done a minimum of three times a year to keep under control. Add wildflower seed and you have a quick and easy nature area. Even better is to put down a perennial 'green manure' a living mulch which also feeds the soil. Some types of clover are very good for this (the Henry Doubleday Research Association (HDRA) has more details).

You will often need to find sources of labour and equipment to clear plots. Work with your Allotments Officer on this one, as they often provide funds for this or offer a plot-clearing service for new plot-holders. You could try applying for general council or other funding. You can then hire what you need. If money is tight, organise a series of volunteer days with your fellow plot holders, or advertise more widely in the local community for help, including your local Volunteer Bureau, community group or environmental group. Offer an incentive, such as plants, produce, or a party afterwards. You will need insurance in case people hurt themselves -

particularly if the site is full of rubbish or if you are using heavy machinery. The British Trust for Conservation Volunteers (BTCV) can provide cheap yearly insurance for groups. They also may be able to provide equipment and voluntary labour hire. Don't forget to make sure you have an up-to-date tetanus jab.

You could also get friendly with alternative sources of labour – the Probation Service or the JobCentrePlus. Or contact your local secondary school – they often run community work programmes. If your management skills are strong and you can offer incentive and training to a team, you may find you empower them and show them a better time than on other placements. This can be contentious though, particularly for JobCentre or Probation placements, and it's really not a good idea if your group is unmotivated and getting nothing out of it. Alternatively, many businesses run 'team building' days, which often involve environmental and community work – if you decide to run one of these, you could charge for it, too!

Advertise
If people don't know something's there, or how to get it, how can they go for it? Allotments often suffer from this. Allotment take-up often works by word of mouth, and this can be very successful for friendly, outgoing sites with attractive plots. However, for people who don't know - or have never known - anyone with a plot, allotments can seem like distant, privately owned gardens operated by members only clubs, and not open to the average punter. This can be particularly true for the many people who have no gardening experience, but would like to learn. They might not even be aware that allotments exist locally.

Advertising is a wonderful way to give people confidence in taking an allotment. Print leaflets and posters advertising the site and allotment gardening generally. Include information on the benefits of growing your own (pesticide and GM-free, exercise, fresh air, sustainability in cities, joys of nature etc), and how to go about getting a plot. Leaflet all local households, doctors' surgeries, supermarkets, health food shops, and local noticeboards, and put posters up all around the site. If you find you enjoy it, you could even produce a site – or an area – newsletter, containing news, events, and contacts.

To further promote your site you could put on an allotments exhibition containing positive images, information, statements, and allotment produce - from flowers to eggs. Shelagh Wilson from the Hastings Federation of Allotment and Leisure Gardeners has put on several successful exhibitions with themes like poverty, and health and diet. The HDRA offers displays for exhibitions and sells leaflets cheaply in bulk for distribution.

Make/clean up the site noticeboard, or better still, make a few, one near each entrance or in prominent positions around the site. Include information on how to get a plot, with contact details, information on local community and allotment projects, amenities and good deals on your site. Change the notices and allotment adverts on it frequently to attract people and make it seem well tended. This can often be easier and as effective as fighting back the brambles on disused plots.

Bristol City Council has displayed colourful and attractive adverts for allotments in the city on the back of buses. As yet, this kind of proactive stance on allotments is rare in local councils. Armed with this example, see if you can encourage your council to do the same.

A very successful project to fill a site was run by Bradford Environmental Action Trust (BEAT), which formed the Allotments Action Group (AAG) in 1993 to rejuvenate allotments in the city. The AAG's first action was to transform a flagging allotment site – Queens Road B – into a vibrant, well-filled one. They chose a site in a busy area so people could actually see it and began an advertising campaign. Producing leaflets and posters, they informed people of the site's existence and how they could go about getting a plot. At the same time, they contacted the local probation service and began to clear plots. Within six months, the site had gone from about 40% take-up to nearly 90% and it is now one of Bradford's show sites.

You could involve your council in many of the ideas mentioned above. Some councils do provide such support. Hopefully, one day it will be part of best practice by all councils to work in partnership with communities and associations to put these basic requirements in place. In the meantime, tell your council what you are up to, and what your needs are, and see what practical and financial help you can get. (Also check the *Sustainability* section in Chapter 5, *Reinvention*.)

Support plot-holders

Gardening should be a pleasure, not a burden. You will keep and increase the number of plot holders by understanding and providing for their needs. New gardeners need support and information to keep them interested – starting a new plot can be a daunting experience and new gardeners can easily be put off.

Share any information you have on gardening – website info and discussion forums, and booklists (or sign them up to the free eco-logic books catalogue!). Distribute leaflets – the HDRA provides useful advice leaflets for new organic gardeners, or make your own.

You could set up a mentoring scheme in which established gardeners work with new ones. This is a good way to mix old and new ideas and unify the whole site. Many younger gardeners lack experience and would love to learn to grow organically. Many older gardeners have the experience to pass on to younger ones, but often not the energy to maintain their plots the way they'd like to.

Some allotment associations and community groups run training sessions for new plot holders. If you do decide to run a course make sure it is well publicised. Even if people don't attend in large numbers it gets out the message that the allotment association is thriving and active. Bath Organic Group run courses on topics of interest to gardeners. Particularly well attended have been those on seed saving, soft fruit growing, pruning and pest control.

A particularly good idea is to hold allotment evenings or work days where a group of people descend on one member's plot and work together for a couple of hours to a plan thought out by the plot-holder. As an added incentive the plot-holder provides the tea and cake (or beer and peanuts). The change is often dramatic and the satisfaction level high. Next time, you work on a different member's plot and so on round the group.

It is important to make people feel welcome, whether or not they've been able to keep up their plot, or muck in with a shared one. Make a point of talking to fellow plot-holders, and helping them out if they need it. These informal networks are one of the pleasures of having an allotment.

Often the stresses of modern life are too much for people and they can't keep up with their plot for various reasons. Don't berate them; offer help or suggestions such as sharing a plot with someone else who is short of time or energy or reducing their plot to a quarter of its original size. Don't forget, the allotment should be a place where such stresses can be forgotten and friendships cultivated.

Tenancy Agreements

You may find it useful to look at and modify your tenancy agreements and constitution. Make the rules relevant and understandable. (Sheffield Organic Food Initiative offers a revised tenancy agreement). Change outdated language or legalese into plain English. You can also change terms like 'rods' and 'poles' to metres. So, rather than the 20-pole standard plot, your allotment would be 1000 square meters. Also offer small plots for new gardeners - half, quarter, or even a tenth of a plot. Decide on rules that you as an association think are relevant, or, if the council provides the agreement, work with them to update it.

Provide amenities

Many people do not take on plots because their needs are not catered for. Some sites are less popular than others because they do not have adequate facilities such as a water supply and toilets. You could do a survey - or get the landlord to - of what facilities each site has. Sites with poor facilities will tend to have more vacancies. Councils are empowered by law to provide basic infrastructure work on sites. Lobby your council for better facilities on sites or improve them yourselves. (See Chapter 5, *Reinvention*, for funding info.)

Toilets can be essential for people who may want to spend time on site. This can be expensive, and plumbing can add to that. Again, there is a low-impact solution – compost toilets. They are sustainable, sanitary, odourless, and produce excellent compost (don't use it directly on your edible plants - it's for trees, comfrey, and borders ... safe to handle, but not to eat!) There is a company which provides disabled access compost toilets (contact Barry Watson for details). An even cheaper DIY solution to this is 'tree bogs'. Bath Organic Group has one on their allotment. They are much less complex than compost loos and just as safe, provided they are well designed and built.

Events

Events are useful for two reasons – they develop unity between plot-holders and can be fantastic advertisements for the site – attracting new plot-holders, community support and free publicity. Everyone can take part in organising, advertising, and providing ideas for events. They're also fun – a good time to let your hair down and forget problems.

Activities such as plant and seed sales, car boot and jumble sales, can raise money for the site. Barbecues or harvest suppers on site in the summer allow people to get to know each other. The annual AGM is a good place for people to socialise as well as sort out site affairs. Include a social as part of it, and maybe a prize draw to attract people. The first AGM I ever went to won me a bottle of gin. That kept me actively involved. Some allotments even have licensed bars! (However, it is worth bearing in mind that some groups and cultures – e.g. Moslems, or recovering alcoholics - do not drink. Depending upon the groups on your site or in your community, you may choose not to base your activities around alcohol.)

If you have developed a new project or piece of shared space on your site (see Chapter 5, *Reinvention*) events are also a wonderful way to attract people and make sure this new initiative is well used. Arts events, and projects, can also be very effective. And don't forget open-air theatre!

In Oxford, a mental health project called Restore covers two acres of an allotment site. It runs a buzzing annual summer festival with bands, DJs, food, stalls, a raffle, and an auction of allotment produce!

The Uplands Allotments in Birmingham held a successful art event on a summer evening in August 1998. Uplands is one of the biggest allotment sites in the country, with 400 plot-holders. They raised £30,000 to run the event, which included flying sheds, poetry, fireworks, and growing umbrellas.

Contact the local and national press – both general and specific interest journals – and publicise your site's projects/sparkly and original events (see Chapter 7, *Campaign*).

Offer good deals/ideas
Try to offer cheap plots to unemployed people, pensioners, or those on low incomes. (Encouraged by the 1950 Allotment Act, many councils do this already.) Free plots in the first year if the plots are incredibly overgrown are also an idea (you could also offer the second year free rather than the first to encourage commitment to the plot).

Shared tool schemes are used by many allotment associations, although often this works informally in practice. It's often simply a matter of introducing people to each other in a friendly setting. Chip in for communal shredders/rotavators and other expensive items. Keep them in a secure lock-up, or a neutral, safe base nearby.

Seed deals
Seeds can be expensive, but saving and swapping seed is a good and easy way to save money, preserve biodiversity, and form good relationships with others. Organise seed sales, buying in bulk and selling cheaply. Many seed companies and horticultural organisations offer good deals. Produce some order forms, organise an event, and let nature take its course.

Bristol's Avon Organic Group (a city-wide horticultural group) holds a yearly seed swap and bulk order through the HDRA, which orders its seed from Chase Organics. They place the order early – in November, which Jon Lucas, the Group's adviser, says is a good thing. 'It ensures you get your seed order in early and sorted out in good time. The seed arrives in time for our January meeting and in February we hold a swap of saved seed and what we have left over from our orders.'

Since, in theory, it is illegal to sell many traditional varieties that don't appear on the National Seed List, swapping seed is the best way, indeed, the only way, to preserve and strengthen ancient local varieties. Bought seeds are often hybrids and won't breed true to type. Not so with the old cultivars. HDRA offers a 'Seed Bank' you could tap into – and then start saving seeds yourself.

Get hold of a copy of *The Seed Savers Handbook* or *Back Garden Seed Saving* from *eco-logic books*; they give excellent instructions on how to save the seed from all the popular herbs and vegetables. Ask older gardeners who may have been saving seed for years, or have tiny 'family heirlooms' tucked away!

Allotments are the perfect places for unofficial seed banks. They often contain a wide range of species and cultivars, all being grown, saved, and swapped by real people producing plants and food they really want to eat. You don't get that with multinational seed companies and large-scale agriculture! You could also work this on a larger inter-site or city, or borough scale. Maybe include discussion in your seed swap-meetings about common cultivar problems and advise those trying new varieties for the first time.

The Sheffield Organic Food Initiative (SOFI) started saving seed to save money and encourage biodiversity. Now they actually make money from the sale of some of the seeds. Richard Clare, who organises their seed bank, says: "Allotments are suitable for seed saving, because you don't need many plants – half a dozen or a dozen plants keep diversity and generate seeds for hundreds of people - so the small scale can influence a larger number of people. We can afford to be generous. A seed bank is a concentrated store of value and potential. A small box is enough for several acres of vegetables. It's like a 'tardis' - it defies the space time continuum."

This section has highlighted some of the basic ways you can improve your site without doing anything too radical (with the possible exception of the compost loo). These ideas and practices pave the way towards a vibrant and popular allotment site, laying the foundations for wider community projects. The next section covers such projects showing ways of involving more people and trying something new.

Reinvent your site

Many thriving allotment sites not only include the traditional 'one person working their plot' system but also wider projects which can involve many different aspects of the local community. Becoming a vibrant community garden or having other projects taking place on site can help to protect allotments from threat as many more local residents take a 'stake' in the site.

Many of these projects play a vital part in community development, in which all kinds of people come together, learning and working alongside each other. They can provide an occupation and a 'place to be' for many who may fall outside the mainstream of society. They can also provide an ideal setting for communication between generations on shared interests. Here the older, experienced gardener can be valued for their gardening wisdom particularly if they are using organic methods. Allotments can also provide training facilities for people on the first step to learning about market gardening and horticulture.

Local Authorities and Sustainability

Because allotments and allotment projects are about gardening, usually in our towns and cities, they are also valuable for the environment. Many of them also have a wider scope than simply vegetable or flower cultivation. This fits them perfectly into sustainability principles, and therefore into council policy, making your Sustainability Officer a perfect ally and source of help for any new project of this nature.

Principles of sustainability were first committed to by the UK government at the 1992 UN Conference on the Environment and Development – the Rio Earth Summit. These principles were enshrined in a crucial document, Local Agenda 21 (LA21), which came out of the Summit. It means, literally, the Agenda for the 21st Century. This is a commitment to sustainable development – development which does not squander or destroy the resources of future generations.

Local Agenda 21 is also a commitment to community and anti-poverty. Because of this, it emphasises activity and change at a local level - combining 'bottom-up' with 'top-down'. In this way, it encourages community groups and individuals to work in partnership with government in the decision-making process.

Agenda 21 is a moral, not a legal agreement. It was signed by almost all the countries attending the Summit (including the UK). The Government expected all councils to have signed up to it by the end of 2000, and all councils are expected to integrate sustainable and community commitments into their policies.

LA21 was further built on at the second World Summit on Sustainable Development in Johannesburg, in 2002, at which the UK Government committed themselves to 'encourage and promote the development of a ten year framework of programmes... to accelerate the shift towards sustainable consumption and production'. This led to the 2003 policy paper *Changing Patterns; UK Government Framework for Sustainable Consumption and Production*, from which a plethora of recent sustainability policies have come.

Sustainable practices are sometimes sidelined by local authorities – they are not seen to be as important as economic or other issues.

However, local authorities usually employ an LA21 Officer, who go by a variety of names – common ones being Sustainability Officer, or Environmental Initiatives Officer. The influence this officer has varies depending upon how committed the local authority is to sustainability. Their position within the council also varies – they could be in Planning departments, Environmental Health departments, Community Development teams, or in a central position in the Chief Executive's office. A lot of authorities have absorbed LA21 posts into their community strategy work. Some councils have whole teams working for sustainability.

A successful sustainability project or campaign is a string to any council's bow. It can bring positive publicity and can show voters and government how sustainable and involving of the community they really are. This win-win situation can be exploited for mutual benefit.

All this makes the LA21, or sustainability office a good place to start for anyone who wants to move towards a more environmentally sustainable community with their allotment site at the heart of it. Make friends with your LA21 Officer. They can help and support you in all aspects of getting sustainable community projects up and running. This could include funding, practical advice, contacts, and expertise. They have the added benefit of working within your local council and so can help navigate round the sometimes bizarre structures and chains of command that exist in some local authorities. Get in touch with them and see how you can work together.

Interesting/alternative projects
In the light of sustainability, unused areas on your allotments do not have to be millstones around your neck. By looking at alternative and sustainable ways of using allotment land, you can turn them round into very positive places from which to begin alternative projects.

The first stage, as mentioned in Chapter 4, is to get talking to interested community groups. These could be Black or Minority Ethnic (BME) groups, women's groups, organic groups, schools, age well, physical and mental health organisations, and composting groups. These groups often take plots and start projects on the site.

Ask your neighbourhood what it wants, and set up meetings inviting attendance from people who want to get involved to shape the new space – throw in some ideas about what could be set up (see *Community Consultation* in Chapter 7, Campaign). You may find that the project begins to take on its own identity, and needs to constitute as a separate entity (go back to Chapter 3, *Organisation*, collect a big merit mark for even thinking about setting up a community project).

The Bolton Wildlife Project has been doing conservation work in and around Bolton since 1990. In 1996 they started a food-growing scheme on allotments and community gardens. The Project now has a seed bank, tool bank, training courses, and a newsletter. Kim Patterson from the Project feels its popularity is easily explainable: 'We're an accessible, down-to-earth project, and we're independent, which is quite useful. People don't see us as an agent of the local authority. It's beautiful because it's informal. If someone needs a work day, other groups come along and lend a hand.'

It is often easier to get the co-operation of your Allotments Officer or other officialdom if you can show them that somebody, somewhere has already done whatever you are proposing (and the world didn't come to an end!) If you have some wacky scheme up your sleeve it may be more productive to talk to the LA21 Officer first or disguise it as something a little less radical.

The ideas below are just some of the most common areas of action that have come my way. Once you open a piece of land to the wider community, and people start buzzing about it, lots of other original ideas may well come up. Remember to start slowly, don't bite off more than you can chew, consider everything, and if it works... well, you could have a 'trailblazer' on your hands!

Community Garden areas

Many sites have space they could turn over to a shared garden area, either for their allotment holders, or the wider community, or for other specific community groups. Shared space for all plot-holders is a good way to encourage community feeling about the site, a place for relaxation, or events. Shared space for specific community groups is also empowering for those groups and can bring new energy to the allotment site.

Community gardens are a very good way of getting many more people involved in gardening and the space around them. They are easier to start up than city farms, as they don't involve the legal and practical complications involved with keeping animals in a community setting (although you can keep animals on allotment sites, with permission, so you may be able to combine the two that way). Some of the most successful community gardens combine shared areas with plots for individual gardening. Community gardens are as diverse as the localities and communities that produce them.

Safe children's and family areas can also be incorporated for the whole community – to widen allotment access and make them available to young and old alike. This is important for allotment holders who are also busy parents, or as a safe and pleasant contemplation area. Elder Stubbs allotments in Oxford have a large pond with willow trees in a corner of their site; a lovely relaxation and contemplation area. Cars on sites can make it a more dangerous place for children to play, so try to separate 'safe' from 'unsafe' areas.

The Federation of City Farms and Community Gardens (the FCF&CG) is a good source of information and help starting up a garden. You may want to create an informal project and not do things by the book, but, depending upon how formal you want to be in your project, the FCF&CG offer a useful starter pack. It contains information on every aspect of setting up a community garden, from funding, to volunteers, health and safety, to insurance. Alternatively, if you start up through an already existing group with paid staff, they could take on these responsibilities for you.

Shared plots

Many people are also living transient lives, and do not have the time to devote the years needed to get a good allotment plot up and running. These people often have the free time to come and help out, particularly if that means they learn something. A shared plot scheme is a perfect way to do that.

Francis Owens, of Teeside Homeless Action says of their allotment and community garden project; 'What's good about the allotment project is that it's nice and easy. People see an end result in a short time. The key is in getting people involved, it doesn't matter how long for. It's doing things and participation that gets people moving again. Because it's creative, it uses a different part of the brain, and shows people that they've got more potential than they thought.' Because homeless people have other things to think about than gardening every week, participation fluctuates: 'Sometimes we have 10 or 12 people come down. The key is to plug away and make sure there's at least one person to maintain the allotment. Usually it's me, because it's dead relaxing.'

Access

Community projects on allotment sites will mean you need to consider access issues, particularly in the initial stages when security is an issue. Many projects do not have open access to non-allotment holders without keys. The way around this is to hold workdays and other events when there are many people around, and the gates are open for the day, or well-publicised and regular 'open days'. Another is to encourage people to become allotment holders, or members of the association.

Sites with poor security – permanently unlocked gates – are often useful for community projects because anyone can come down, but this does not always benefit the rest of the site. Unknown people wandering around the site can upset existing plot holders and if your site is locked it's often best to have named key holders rather than giving everyone a key.

Allotments are interesting spaces – private areas open to all. Access is always an issue with community projects, and, indeed, the debate rages as to whether allotments should be locked to non-allotment holders at all. It's best not to get involved in that one, methinks.

Permaculture

In the early 1970s, the term permaculture (permanent agriculture plus sustainable culture) was coined by two Australians, Bill Mollison and David Holmgren. Permaculture is all about designing sustainable systems and includes horticulture as a large component. To try to

condense a global philosophy into a couple of lines is impossible.
Mike Feingold, Bristol-based Permaculture teacher, says:
'Permaculture is revolution dressed up as gardening.'

You may recognise some of the ideas that have entered common
currency which are based on permaculture principles, for example,
forest gardening. This simple but effective idea makes use of
perennial plants and trees incorporated within good design to create
a self-sustaining, low-maintenance area of land.

You could design a whole allotment site or part of one along
permaculture lines. You might include an orchard area, a chicken run
– fed in summer by surrounding it with growing chicken delights, a
compost area etc. These ideas are dependent upon a shared vision of
gardening, and may not be useful for more traditional sites; although
you could incorporate individual vegetable plots in your design. You
could have loads of fun with this - a good place to start is to read
Graham Bell's Permaculture Garden and contact the Permaculture
Association for a list of courses in your area.

The Bath Organic Group has taken several plots and merged them as
one along permaculture lines, removing the paths and reshaping the
area as a permaculture garden. Lovely stuff and well worth a visit.

Alternative crops

The UK climate permits growing plants from all around the world.
This can make for a more varied and interesting diet and is very
good for inter-ethnic communication and learning. Some examples
of successful crops are Asian coriander, West Indian calaloo, Chinese
pakchoy, Japanese squash, and Indian corn. The Sheffield Organic
Food Initiative has more details.

Non-food crops, particularly willow for basket-making, could also
run in tandem with special interest/needs-based projects. Such crops
are especially important if your site is contaminated. You will usually
need the agreement of the council or your allotments association to
grow perennials as tree crops. Plants for a Future provide a database
of interesting, rare plants useful to humans often as non-food crops

such as soap, dyes, and textiles. Bees, chickens and rabbits are huge fun and can all also be kept on allotments. Bristol City Council even allows goats on one or two sites – with permission.

Trees and orchards

You could start a community orchard on a vacant part of your allotment, and contemplate to your heart's content amidst the trees. Community orchards are perfect for allotments since they combine food growing with a garden area. The charity, Common Ground, has been successfully promoting the growing and eating of local apple varieties for years. Contact them for advice on everything from running an Apple Day celebration to the latest community projects, or check their book, The Common Ground Book of Orchards, also available from eco-logic books.

You can grow willow for local basket-makers and basket-making projects. This is particularly good for poor soil or contaminated areas. Willow sculpture is also trendy and fun. You can make seats and fencing and decorative bits for your garden area. Remember to get the sculpture pruned regularly or it will lose all its shape.

Again, you generally need permission from the site owner to plant orchard trees. The up side is that they are often sympathetic to the idea of letting you have the plots at a reduced or nil rent. If you don't ask, you don't get.

Several plots in Bradford are being used as a tree nursery as part of the Forest of Bradford project, backed by the council. Because the allotments are simply being used as a 'holding bay' for the trees, the council is fine with it. The Bradford Community Environment Project has more details.

Health

We all know how therapeutic gardening can be, how the exercise, fresh air and organic vegetables they produce can benefit body and mind. This can make health-centred projects very attractive, and, indeed, they are becoming more common on allotments. Government policy is now encouraging healthier eating and exercise, which means that local Health Authorities will very often support, or run, allotment projects. This is particularly useful if specialist healthcare workers are required for such a scheme, and you can work in partnership with larger organisations who can help run the project with you. Alternatively, you could make those connections and 'offer up' an unused portion of your site for such a scheme to run.

Peter Driver, of the proactive Hastings and St Leonard's Allotment Federation, became an allotment rep on the Hastings Health Authority's '5 a Day' pilot project in 2000. 'We said "5 a Day" was not just about eating more fruit and veg. It was about actually being able to grow your own, organic food, in the fresh air, in a community setting, which brings mental benefits, plus the physical benefits of exercise and healthy eating.' Says Peter. 'Allotments have got so much to offer, they couldn't refuse to take it up.' As a result of this input, the '5 a Day' project recruited a Food Growing Worker and began two community projects on allotment sites.

Bradford Community Environment Project in partnership with the local Health Authority run a project through the Bradford Food Network, called Sho Nibar (Bangladeshi for 'Self Reliance') on allotments in Bradford. The project is for Bangladeshi women and men, amongst whom the incidence of heart disease is high. It was started in 1999 to promote exercise and healthy eating through gardening – and has won an award for its success.

Ecoworks in Nottingham is based on the permaculture principle, 'Earth Care, People Care'. It aims to integrate mental health with environmental activities. Their Garden Project on the Hungerhill allotments comprises eight plots and combines volunteers who have used mental health services with environmentally minded volunteers. Paul Paine, Garden Project Worker says: 'The process of growing and working together is as important as the yields harvested. There is no distinction between different volunteers, and everybody, whatever they contribute, creates a community that is greater than the sum of its parts.'

Thrive, previously called Horticultural Therapy, are involved with setting up many gardening projects for people with mental or physical disabilities. They are a good source of help and advice in starting up new ventures and supporting existing ones.

Environmental education

Recent government policy on health and schools encourages healthy eating and exercise. Combine this with a rising concern about obesity amongst schoolchildren and commitment to sustainability, and, again, allotments come out on top. In the past few years, allotment sites and projects are finding they don't need to reach out to local schools, instead finding that schools are increasingly coming to them. Many allotment associations set plots aside for environmental education, to involve local schools and the community.

Hartcliffe Health & Environment Actions Group (HHEAG) runs several successful school growing projects in Bristol. Project Manager, Sue Walker gives a reason for their success: 'The schools we work with all have an enthusiastic key member of staff. This is vital for any co-operative project to ensure organisation and continuity.'

HHEAG school projects include gardening clubs for primary school children, plus horticulture training leading to qualifications for a secondary school. 'The value of gardening and the environment are not recognised in the National Curriculum and not considered cool with young people.' Says Sue: 'At about 15, many young people lose interest. However, I've found with environmental work that after ten or fifteen years, something rings a bell, and they often return to it remembering all the old skills and knowledge. Having said that, with gardening programmes on TV and the cult of the personality, gardening is a bit more sexy now!'

Although gardening and horticulture are not recognised in the National Curriculum, they contain many of the vital ingredients for it, including the sciences, particularly biology; maths, English, and even history and geography. Often schools do not have the space for vegetable gardens, but a local allotment site can be perfect, and eventually involve parents too. The National Curriculum can be restrictive about time allocated to gardening projects, but working through schools, and creating one-off workdays which lead to after-school clubs, or school holiday activities can often be the way to go. It is often easier to start projects in primary schools as the curriculum is more flexible.

The Moulsecoomb Forest Garden and Wildlife Project in Brighton offers free allotment activities for children in summer holidays and tours for schools. Kim, a Project Worker, explains: "We do a 'taste and smell' tour, which kids love, because most of them don't know what the vegetables are. Some of them don't know that they're grown in the ground. They love it so much, romping around in the mud, finding beasties. Once the kids are involved it's a good way to draw the parents in."

The Federation of City Farms and Community Gardens has a wealth of information about schools and food growing. Contact them for details of government policy and flagship projects.

Wildlife areas

A very good way of promoting a site's environmental importance and of involving more community and environmental groups is to create a wildlife area. Allotments are often the only green oasis for miles around and it can be a simple and satisfying process to join together with local birdwatchers, environmental groups and schools to build on that fact. It has got to be easier to turn a thoroughly disused and be-brambled couple of plots into a wildlife sanctuary than to struggle to turn them into plots that are never going to amount to much.

Take a tip from the permaculturalists' book and observe your site well before you charge in with radical changes. Some pieces of land, like those north-facing bits behind a large hedge are just not meant for vegetables but are ideal wildlife habitats. Often, as in the case of slow-worms, important wildlife and well-managed plots work symbiotically together, so you don't need or want separate areas. Yours could become a showcase allotment - wildlife and gardeners improving the eco-system and coexisting.

Ponds

No wildlife habitat or indeed orchard or community garden is complete without a pond. Pond building can be a deeply satisfying activity. Ponds attract insects, amphibians, foxes, birds and small children in vast numbers. Pond building as an activity has many of the factors needed for a successful project – several people can be involved with different levels of skill, the result is achieved relatively quickly and is there for all to see. With any pond or water feature you need to be sensitive to the safety element. Ponds act as magnets to children and left without supervision or some form of safety barrier, accidents can be fatal. That said, there is nothing more satisfying than having a shared summer picnic by the pond you built yourselves.

Local Food Links

Local Food Links are about completing the circle from plot to plate. Often this simply means enabling farmers to sell straight to consumers cheaply and without middlemen. But there's a strong community component to it too. It's about making links on every level, and allotments are a very important part of this. Community cafés, breakfast clubs for school children and lunch clubs for pensioners, cooking clubs – are all part of Local Food Links. It also involves bulk food buying and sourcing locally produced food – which could include your allotment. Highlighting social and economic issues by taking part in such a scheme scores big points with councils or funding bodies.

Community composting

This is often an ideal activity for an allotment site and gets many green stars as an environmental activity. Relatively easy to set up (check the Community Composting Network for help and advice) – green waste is either collected from local households or bought by householders to the site where it is dealt with. A big bonus of setting up such a scheme is the compost a group can produce. This can either be given back or sold to the donors or used to improve often depleted allotment soil cheaply and organically. Although relatively easy to set up, composting schemes can be harder to keep going as they require regular, guaranteed commitment – a slight hiccup in the personnel department can lead to piles of rotting vegetation and there is nothing like the sweet smell of putrefaction to upset people living right next to it.

The Bolton Wildlife Project set up a scheme in 1998 on seven plots which involves taking compost from the about 35 households every week in return for a box of vegetables every fortnight. The scheme also relies upon volunteers to come and help out, again, in return for vegetables.

Funding

The best and most sustainable plots are always self-funding; however, funding is an area where community groups come into their own – as they can often get funding where councils can't. It can be very productive to use new projects to attract funding - there are a multitude of small and large funders for interesting local projects.

Start by seeing what funds area available from local organisations or your council, and work upwards, gathering information on new funding sources along the way. Many of the organisations listed in the contacts list will be able to help you with advice on good funding bodies. There is also some software, FunderFinder, which pinpoints donors for specific projects – ring around your local community organisations for access.

Each donor is different; some don't want any contact except a one-page letter outlining your project, with a few supporting documents. Others want you to fill in a detailed application form. It sounds crazy but a high proportion of bids fail and are rejected because they don't give the funder what they have asked for.

It's relatively easy to get money for single things like training, equipment, and materials. It can be harder to get 'core funding' – general office running costs, salaries, that kind of thing. Remember, once you've got the money it's no good spending it on a trip to Cuba. You will need to account for every penny. However, be truthful, and down to earth, always over-estimate costs, and you should get just about what you need. Allotments, with their sustainability and community aspects, sell themselves.

A sad but true fact is that the less contentious a project is the easier it is to attract funding. You can always get money to plant trees and dig ponds whereas raising money for a performance poet to hold daily readings in a shed on your allotment can be a tad more difficult. Check the contacts list – there are some fantastic publications out there that can give you loads more help than I ever can.

Many allotment projects and associations fall into the trap whereby they don't do anything without funding. Many fold because funding dries up. Try not to find yourselves in this position. A strong community project should not need to rely upon money to keep going.

Kim, from the Moulsecoomb Forest Garden and Wildlife Project says: 'We went five years without funding. We have been funded for three years, and two of us have got part-time jobs now, and we do so much more than we did before. We have talked about what would happen if we lose our funding. We would carry on because of the dedication of the group. We've made a commitment to keep it going; we'll all do one day's voluntary work. You've got to love it, not just as a job. You've got to be a gardener.'

Look into how you can make your own money from your own resources. Can you hire out your clubhouse for parties, or your site to art groups? Site shops are a common way to raise funds, as are benefit gigs, raffles, and jumble sales. Be inventive.

Barmpton Lane Allotment Association is in the process of planting 200 Christmas trees to raise funds for the site. Michael Haw, Association Chair, says: 'The funds will go towards reducing rents of present plot-holders. As a self-managed site, we submit an annual plan to the council, which this year included the Christmas tree plantation. The council are absolutely delighted that we're utilising a piece of land which couldn't be used in any other way.'

With a bit of lateral thinking you can often do many things cheaply yourself. Much of the alternative green movement is based around this idea – it's called DIY Culture. It's just a reinvention of the way people have always done things. Add the four Rs – Reduce, Reuse, Repair, Recycle – and be inventive and original in what you do, you can save money and will not need to rely so heavily on funding.

Greer Hart, of the Queens Park Allotments, Glasgow, uses old plastic from bus shelters and reclaimed wood and bricks to make greenhouses for the site. He is inventive and original in sourcing materials and has many different ways of fundraising or saving money. 'You've got to source your contacts and quite jealously guard them. If there's too many people on the scene, the source dries up.' He says: 'If you're on the streets at night, you can find things people have thrown out. All sorts of stuff – plastic containers, timber, doors for greenhouses, I build up a supply. That's what I do; I'm a scavenger.'

It is an easy trap to fall into, relying on money and funding for all your needs. Try to see money as just one aspect of the whole. Consume less and be stronger and more self-reliant.

Contamination

This is a nasty section which doesn't fit anywhere easily. Some sites provided for allotments in Victorian times were old dumps or disused factory works, and not desirable for further use by those who owned them. This has created a problem on some allotments of heavy metal contamination. There is no easy answer to land contamination, or many, depending upon which way you look at it.

There are two sources of information you might find useful on contamination. Firstly, The Scottish Allotment and Gardens Society, who have recently experienced issues with contamination and worked alongside local government on this, as well as producing an information leaflet on the issue for allotment holders. Secondly, the booklet *Growing Food: How Safe is Your Land?* is the only publication on contamination for community food growers, available on the Internet or from the North West Food and Health Task Force (see *Bibliography*).

If you want your site preserved for open space, but no longer for cultivation for consumption, what do you do? You can import fresh soil, or grow in raised beds, or grow bushes which don't take up the slow-moving metals. Lime your soil, as an alkaline soil also helps slow take-up. The issue of importing soil is one you should be able to get the council to move on. Try to highlight the fact that the contamination is their responsibility. This is also a time when the dreaded developer comes into their own – almost all development produces topsoil, which is often landfilled, although the sustainable option would be to recycle it and use it on your plot (test the topsoil for contaminants first, though). People have used impermeable membranes to cap the undesirable soil, and then imported 15-30cms of topsoil.

Barry Watson has produced his own DIY solution to dodgy ground, or lack of soil. Working on top of rubble on an old bombsite, he imported huge amounts of leaves from the University of East London and produced a quality growing-medium from it, calling it his 'makings'. As this is literally pure compost, it is so soft, potatoes can be literally picked from the plant, and the roots re-covered. The plants love it!

Growing non-vegetable crops such as flowers, natural dye, or willow for basket-making means you will need a market and to get the use changed for your site. However, bear in mind the information in *Redefining your allotment,* below.

Surplus produce

The 1922 Act defines an allotment garden as 'wholly or mainly cultivated by the occupier for the production of vegetable or fruit crops for consumption by himself or his family.'

People often ask whether they can sell what they produce from an allotment. The answer, according to the above law is, well, yes, some of it, but the law is designed to ensure that allotments are not put to commercial use. Community use is fine, but you can't operate a business from a plot. However, the word 'mainly', in the legal text provides loopholes and is fuzzy in definition. This tends to be defined as selling surplus produce. As an example, Bristol City Council sets as 49% of what you grow as surplus. There is no case law on prosecutions against anyone for selling allotment produce. Farmers' Markets are also fast becoming an acceptable way of selling surplus produce, as they are part of Local Food Links, benefiting the local community (or 'family', if you like!)

The commercial use of allotments could threaten the position of those who want to cultivate them for personal consumption. Occasionally, councils do let out parts of sites for commercial use – the issue is whether they get an appropriate rent. You could try changing the

---

definition of the use if you want to use any part of the site for commercial enterprise (see *Redefining your allotment*, below). Make sure it reverts to allotments if you ever leave the site.

Surplus food can also be donated to charity, local soup kitchens for the homeless, or sold at farm shops or Farmers' Markets. These markets are springing up in towns all over the country and are an integral part of Local Food Links. Contact the Soil Association or the National Farmers' Retail and Markets Organisation for more details. Bath Organic Group (BOG) has a permanent place in the hugely successful Bath Farmers' Market. Once a month members can bring their surplus produce from garden or allotment to sell at the market. The system is simple and effective and can provide a handy source of income for both the grower and the local group.

Redefining your allotment

If all or part of your allotment site is derelict and there is no demand for allotments, but there is a general will to change it into something else, such as a community market garden, or wildlife park, you will need to redefine its use in a new tenancy agreement.

Section 27(5) of the 1908 Act makes provision for a site to be leased temporarily for other purposes (i.e. if it's not to be 'wholly or mainly cultivated by the occupier for the production of vegetable or fruit crops for consumption by himself or his family'), as long as it reverts to allotment cultivation should allotment sites be required. It is important to set up a lease agreement between the management authority and the new user using this legislation, if necessary, otherwise the allotment could lose statutory protection. This legislation could also be used to accommodate group use not covered by a standard tenancy agreement.

If the site is privately owned, and without planning permission, it would be relatively cheap, and you could apply for funding to buy the site (a site without planning permission could be worth several tens or hundreds of thousands of pounds, as opposed to several million with permission). National Lottery funding would be a good source for this. Also check the National Playing Fields Society in the contacts list. You would need to fulfil the requirements of the funding body you applied to and probably show that the site was going to be used for community benefit.

You will need to make sure any non-allotment land you have a stake in has the same, or better protection as allotment land. Invest the land in a trust, a co-operative, an association or another public body that will help to protect it from future development or speculation. You may also want to include in the constitution some arrangement that would revert the land to allotments once demand for it in its current state had waned, or when demand for allotments picked up again. However, no association, whatever constitution it has, can protect a site from the planners - it cannot be guaranteed that future trustees will not change the constitution and their rights. It is possible, in the case of a charitable trust, to make legal arrangements so that its constitution cannot be changed without the consent of the Charity Commissioners, or even the local authority.

Allotments and sustainable land use

Looking at this section, you will have seen that many of the ideas and practices that thriving local allotment projects have in common is that they expand the nature of allotment gardening. This not only includes the diversity of people and activities involved, but also what is grown and added to allotment sites.

Interestingly (and possibly not surprisingly), this harks back to the original ways allotments were used. At the turn of the century, there were many different types of allotment. They included fuel (firewood), field (grazing), and gardens (vegetable growing). The 1950 Act changed this and obliged local councils only to provide allotment gardens. If you look at all parts of land use - trees for coppicing and firewood, animals for consumption and manure, and fruit and vegetables, you can see them as part of a sustainable trinity.

The definition of the 'modern' allotment garden, restrictive as to what can be grown and how it can be used, have made allotments dependent upon external inputs, and therefore often difficult and off-putting to cultivate, and in many ways unsustainable. This sustainability issue is an important point to keep in mind when and if you are considering different ways of using parts of your site, as well as being a positive idea which fits neatly into principles of sustainability. Within existing allotments legislation, we are limited to what we can do with the 'derelict' land available but, as we have seen, it is possible to challenge this positively and constructively, in ways which are popular with local councils and your community.

However, on a slightly less positive note, this sustainable framework is under threat (shock!). The current practice of allowing development on whole or parts of currently derelict allotment sites is a dangerous path to take if we wish to retain this original holistic way of doing things. Maybe not all the land on your site is suitable for traditional vegetable cultivation, because of its position within the site as a whole. However, this does not mean that it can't become a useful, or indeed, central part of your allotments, whilst still retaining maximum space for vegetable cultivation. The next two sections will show how you can challenge threats to that land, so you, too, will be able to build that compost toilet (and everything else that goes with it).

Protection

We all hope it will never happen but, as a tenant with no security of tenure from one year to the next, allotmenteers need to know what to do in the face of eviction. It's vitally important to know the status of your allotment site in local plans, so you can act as early as possible to challenge any potential danger to the site. A threat could turn out to be a blessing if it arouses people to action and to realise the value of allotment sites which could be lost.

This section covers the basic legal background to your case. If you discover your site is under threat, don't panic or do or say anything in the public arena until you are familiar with the details of your own case. This section is split into two – the first half on legal issues of sale and development as related specifically to allotments, and the second half on planning issues generally. The next section on campaigning will then take you through what to do when you have this information.

Allotment sale and development

One of the main issues in the sell-off of allotment land is whether the site is temporary or permanent. This will mean different campaign tactics.

Statutory sites

Owned by the local authority. They have legal protection and cannot be sold unless it can be proved that the site is derelict or that there is no demand for it. Only then can the Secretary of State authorise its sale for development.

The Government Response to the 1998 Select Committee report underlined requirements that local authorities should consult with plot-holders before disposing of land. It pointed to general government legislation on wider local authority consultation and felt that this was also very relevant to allotments.

The Government also pre-empted the Select Committee report and introduced a new policy requirement in March 1998 before the production of the Committee's final recommendations. This was: '...a requirement for local authorities to demonstrate the steps they have taken to promote allotments in their area before they can obtain the Secretary of State's consent to dispose of statutory allotment land ...the extent of promotion is taken into account when assessing the extent of local demand for allotments.'

Your Local Agenda 21 Officer can be very useful to you when dealing with council sell-off. They may have access to valuable information and inside knowledge of the council. They may also be able to help you to lobby the right people in the council.

Temporary and private sites

In theory, you have no legal protection whatsoever for temporary or private sites. They were set up so that private owners, or councils (which tend to own temporary sites), could provide allotments rather than letting land they had bought for some unspecified future venture go to waste. As a result, there are few rights for tenants on temporary allotments, and even fewer for those on private sites.

Do not despair – this then becomes entirely a planning issue, and you can fight it, often successfully, on these grounds. Councils may well be happy to block planning permission on privately owned sites as they don't stand to make anything from the sale of the site, and it looks good for them to save a popular environmentally important area. Additionally, a good case with strong community backing could embarrass a council into retaining a temporary site (Chapter 7, *Campaign*, can help with this).

There are also many crossover issues which apply to all allotment sites, but which will affect sites differently depending upon their status.

Eviction notices

On temporary and statutory sites, you cannot be evicted without twelve months' notice, expiring on or before 6 April, on or after 29

SIMPLE QUESTIONS FOR LOCAL PLANNING OFFICIALS:
❶ Which is the most efficient provider of cheap food for the local community?

ⓐ **AN ALLOTMENT SITE** or ⓑ **A NEW SUPERMARKET**

September (Section 1 of the 1922 Act, as amended by Section One of the 1950 Act). Under the 1922 Act, three months' notice can be given for building, mining, or other industrial purpose, or for roads or sewers.

For private sites, the grounds for eviction will be outlined in the lease signed between plot-holders and the landowner. This is called a break clause, and the standard break clause in private leases tends to echo the language of the law: three months' notice is given for 'building, or other industrial purpose'.

Many plot-holders, when threatened with eviction notices, ignore them and continue working their plots. Most of the time, the landowner seeking development ignores this (this happened with both the Telferton and Spitalcroft Allotments sites – more details on their battles follow). However, in the case of St Stephen's Allotment Society in Bath, when plot-holders defied an eviction notice served by the Diocese of Bath and Wells, on one level, this went against them.

Vic Finlayson, Secretary of the Society, says: 'We kept the plots cultivated through thick and thin, we told everyone all along, you must not give up your plot, no matter what, we persuaded them all to stick with us. We were served with an eviction notice at a very early stage. We were all served with eviction notices with 12 months' notice, and at the end they didn't do anything. Then, in the end, five of our people got court summonses – three of the plot-holders were very old. One had just come out of hospital with a heart condition. The court said that they had to pay costs, which came to nearly a thousand pounds. When we came out of court we were stunned, because we had been told that they would not ask for costs, and we had to find nearly a thousand pounds. There were reporters waiting outside the court and they all asked us "What are you going to do?" We said: "If the people of Bath want this land they must help us" and we started getting money through the post. The National Society also gave us a generous contribution and the plot-holders didn't have to pay a penny.'

If you have been served with an eviction notice without planning permission having been obtained for the land, Charlie Hopkins of EarthRights Solicitors argues that that the tenancy termination is unlawful because the landowners do not have the right to occupy the land - they have no reason to do so. This does not apply to private sites – permission to occupy the land comes down to the specific wording of the lease agreement. However, the landowners must prove they own the land, which is sometimes difficult to do!

If the landlord/developer has issued you with an eviction notice, and gone through all the 'proper channels' to reclaim the land, it is worth bearing in mind that in the majority of cases planning permission – i.e. change of use, is needed to trash a site - remove topsoil, bulldoze it, etc.

Developers will however, often come on to a site and illegally begin works on it anyway. This tactic was successfully used on Royate Hill (a non-allotment site) in Bristol in 1992 by a company who wanted to build on a site but make sure it had no wildlife value beforehand. If you are unsure of the developer's tactics, it may be worth keeping your eye on the site after you have been served with eviction notices. (The New York City campaign to save their community gardens distributed hundreds of fridge magnets with a telephone number and the words: 'Bulldozer Hotline, call any time, day or night').

If developers do try to destroy the site without planning permission, use your campaign to highlight their tenuous legal position. When the developers at Royate Hill returned on a Bank Holiday weekend to further trash the site the campaigners physically blocked the bulldozers. This was the start of a successful campaign to turn the area into a local nature reserve. Councils have the power to seek injunctions for this sort of thing. There are also such things as Stop Notices and, soon to come into force, Temporary Stop Notices, which local planning departments can issue, if the illegal possession is brought to their attention.

Parish and Town Councils (Community Councils in Wales) have the power to raise a rate for anything that is to the benefit of the parish and parishioners. This could be useful in something like the above to raise the funds for a challenge or injunction. At the Manchester Airport Second Runway one parish council raised £130,000 as a rate to go to the European Court.

However, continuing to tend your plots or lying in front of bulldozers when an eviction notice has expired can still involve a risk. You may want to seek legal advice first. (See *Direct Action* at the end of Chapter 7, Campaign). In the case of St Stephen's, this form of direct action was successful, because it kept morale up and won their case – they used it as part of their campaign, and it showed how many people supported them. At Royate Hill, they literally saved their site in this way. Both actions proved how important the site was to local people and how the land could be seen as their land, and in the end they won anyway. Be prepared to challenge unlawful evictions and activities - be brave and go for it! As Jean Finlayson, also involved in the campaign adds: "That Summons was the last desperate gambit of the Diocese - there was a sense that we were winning when they tried to do such a desperate thing."

Dereliction
Some councils will not let out plots on sites they have earmarked for development, even though sell-off has not yet been agreed to by the

Secretary of State. In this way, many local authorities have been known to deliberately 'run down' allotments to prove a lack of demand for the Secretary of State. This is illegal, but it is can be difficult to get around. A determined council will put up all kinds of obstacles to ensure site development. It is important to establish the council's motives. Are they admitting that there's no demand and that the site is earmarked for development or are they keeping quiet about their future plans? Is the site full or not? Get a number of people to phone up requesting plots, to see whether the council is letting plots.

Local authorities cannot refuse you an allotment if you are a resident of the area and allotments are available, but it doesn't matter where you live to take an allotment in your chosen area. Garner states: "If a prospective tenant considers he has been unfairly passed over in the matter of allocation of tenancies, he should complain to his councillor, and if this does not satisfy him, he may consider asking the councillor to refer the complaint, alleging an act of 'maladministration' to the Local Government Commissioner for Administration under the Local Government Act 1974, part III." This could mean using the District Auditor or Local Government Ombudsman to investigate the situation, (bearing in mind that the Ombudsman can be very slow, and has no power to order a Council to do anything). Similarly, this is an argument which private landowners can use to win planning permission – they serve eviction notices before they have applied for planning permission in order to show that the site is derelict. Don't be fooled. (And don't stop working your plot - see above!)

Ian Goodbrand, of Telferton Allotments, Edinburgh, who won their case last year, after five years, says: "Bett Homes (the prospective developers) were trying to prove that the land was derelict. It wasn't derelict. The allotments had been in existence for over 100 years – used by local people which included many ethnic minorities and a community garden group." They continued to use the site, and made the case for the site popularity in the court case, which they won.

Compensation for lost sites

Replacement sites

Before granting disposal of allotment land, the law states that the Secretary of State must be satisfied that 'adequate provision will be made for allotment holders displaced by the action of the local authority or that such provision is unnecessary or not reasonably practicable.' (Section 8 of the Allotments Act, 1925). This is a very important point which has been successfully used in campaigns.

The Government's Response to the 1998 Select Committee Report added to this by stating that 'Replacement sites are required not normally to be more than three quarters of a mile from the centre of demand, although this distance may be increased if the plot-holders are willing to travel further.'

Chris Carver, Friends of the Earth campaigner, and the brains behind the campaign to save Spitalcroft Allotments, Devizes, argued her case on the grounds that "The alternative site had to be as convenient and productive as the original one. The one we were offered was on top of a hill above the highest roof in the town – completely exposed and under mobile phone masts. It would have been useless, and it had been put to grassland. The site visit was the determining factor. The inspector could not fold his map, it was so windy up there!" If you are in a similar situation, Chris suggests that you "Find out what grade of land you've got – we've got Grade 1 land." If the alternative site is not up to scratch, work that into your campaign. Do bear in mind, though, that the definition 'adequate' in the 1925 Act can be taken to mean just that – even if it isn't as good as your original site.

The 1908 Act states that councils have to plough all, or a reasonable percentage of the revenue they make from the sale of allotments back into allotment provision. The surplus can be used elsewhere in the council. Since how much to be spent on allotments is left to councils, this gives them some leeway, but councils usually take this requirement into account.

Another useful financial tool for communities are legal agreements drawn up after planning permission has been agreed for a private developer. Previously called Section 106 agreements, (now scrapped under the new planning law, see below), they are money and services provided by the developer to mitigate the effects of the impacts of the development. Sometimes councils use money from the developers to plough into projects which are actually unrelated to the development - so keep an eye out for this. However, it can mean that if a developer takes a piece of green space in a city, they must also provide money for urban open space provision locally.

Financial compensation

There is a legal requirement on local councils to relocate or offer recompense to tenants evicted from a sold-off site (from 1950 Act). A legal precedent for compensation exists in housing law for council tenants when they have to move to another council property (for instance due to remodelling of an estate). Compensation or payoffs are sometimes used as an inducement to encourage tenants to move off a site (if there was collusion between councils and developers).

Planning policies

Any change in the use of a piece of land (called 'development' whether or not anything substantial is built upon it) needs planning permission. To block any form of development, you therefore need knowledge of the planning system, because it is this you will be working within in any campaign.

The planning system has changed radically with the introduction of the Planning and Compulsory Purchase Act 2004. The information below is applicable in England only. In Wales, Scotland and Northern Ireland the planning system is similar in that there are National Spatial Strategies for you to get involved in for each of these countries. Use the contacts list for organisations which can guide you through.

The new Act abolishes Local Plans, Structure Plans, and Regional Guidance, and replaces them with Regional Spatial Strategies (RSS), and Local Development Frameworks (LDF). Planning on a local level is changing to be more involving of local communities, with more emphasis on sustainability. The problem is, however, that RSS are being designed by

Regional Assemblies, which, apart from London, are not elected bodies. Since Local Development Frameworks have to conform to RSS many lobby groups argue that this is unaccountable, and undemocratic.

It is essential that you have knowledge of what has been planned for your region by making yourself aware of the content of your RSS. In particular, check to see if your area is planned to be designated as a Business Growth Zone, as this designation will have a major impact. Check also Regional Planning Guidance for your area, available through your Regional Government Office (contact the ODPM or check its website for details). It is possible to get involved in the development of these strategies by contacting your council for contact details, or obtaining them from a web search of Regional Assemblies. Ask your Regional Assembly to put you on their database and keep you informed of developments so you can comment. You have a legal right to put in a written submission to your Regional Assembly commenting on the RSS.

Get involved in your Local Development Framework, and get in early, as this way you will be guaranteed to have an impact. Unlike RSS, community consultation is built into the development of LDF – local authorities are expected to listen to your opinions on this. Check to see what has been planned for allotments and/or open space in your area. Many local authorities are now producing allotment strategies. If yours has, compare and contrast to see how one can influence the other.

At the time of writing (early 2005), The Planning and Compulsory Purchase Act is brand new, and not in force in its entirety. Some lobbyists argue that it is inconsistent. Although much of the decision making for regional planning is now being decided at a top level without mandatory community consultation, there are other ways you will be able to mount challenges. Using the Human Rights Act and the Aarhus Convention to challenge decisions on their legality is one way. Additionally, local authorities may support you in challenges, because Regional Assemblies have eroded their powers.

Because this planning system is so new, you are strongly advised to use the planning section of the contacts list, particularly the

Campaign for Planning Sanity, and the Town and Country Planning Association.

Planning Policy Guidance Notes and Statements

Planning Policy Guidance Notes (PPGs) are government planning policies. There are 24 of them. They are revised from time to time (and numbers are re-used as certain titles become defunct), so make sure you get up-to-date copies. They should all be available in all main libraries.

With the Planning and Compulsory Purchase Act, PPGs are being replaced by Planning Policy Statements (PPSs), which are supposed to make policy more concise and easier to understand. The numbers are the same, and PPSs will replace PPGs as they are produced, PPS come with accompanying guidance notes for help with interpretation.

By law, all planning must be guided by what is set out in the PPGs and PPSs. They cannot be ignored but they are not to be followed strictly as other competing issues may outweigh those policies. You can't sue for non-compliance with a PPG, but you can seek Judicial Review of the planning application if the planner or local authority haven't taken it into account.

You can challenge a planning application by showing how it is not in line with the relevant PPG. This happens quite a lot. PPGs can often be vague and open to interpretation. The trick is to interpret them in your way and stick to it. Remember PPGs are only one part of the bigger picture (more on this in the next chapter).

Local Authorities also issue Supplementary Planning Guidance (SPG), similar to PPGs and PPSs – additional guidance on specific policy topic areas. This is useful for campaigners as SPG are about to become legally binding under the new LDF.

In addition to this, planning policy is supplemented by Circulars, which give advice on legislation and procedures. There are many other government briefing papers and codes of practice that supplement the general policies. Most planning policy documents can be downloaded from the Planning Portal (www.planningportal.gov.uk).

Planning Policy Guidance Notes:

PPG1   General Policy and Principles
PPG2   Green Belts
PPG3   Housing
PPG4   Industrial & Commercial Development & Small Firms
PPG5   Simplified Planning Zones
PPG6   Town Centres and Retail Developments
PPS7   Sustainable Development in Rural Areas
PPG8   Telecommunications
PPG9   Nature Conservation
PPG10 Planning and Waste Management
PPS11 Regional Spatial Strategies
PPG12 Local Development Frameworks
PPG13 Transport
PPG14 Development on Unstable Land
PPG15 Planning and the Historic Environment
PPG16 Archaeology and Planning
PPG17 Sport and Recreation
PPG18 Enforcing Planning Control
PPG19 Outdoor Advertisement Control
PPG20 Coastal Planning
PPG21 Tourism
PPS22 Renewable Energy
PPS23 Planning and Pollution Control
PPG24 Planning and Noise
PPG25 Development and Flood Risk

Unlike legal statutes, PPG and PPS are easy to read, with clear headings. The most useful for allotment holders are:

■ **PPG1: General Policy and Principles** – Useful to begin your research. States that sustainability is the cornerstone of current planning policy, for example. At the time of writing, this is about to be replaced by PPS1, which has a stronger commitment to sustainable development and community involvement.

■ **PPG2: Green Belts** – which outlines the development restrictions in green belts.

■ **PPG3: Housing** – Revised in March 2000. Finally clearing up the wrangle over that definition of allotments, it contains a definition of 'brownfield', or previously developed land, which *excludes land and buildings that are currently in use for agricultural or forestry purposes, and land in built-up areas which has not been developed previously (e.g. parks, recreation grounds, and allotments - even though these areas may contain certain urban features such as paths, pavilions and other buildings). It also says; Developing housing in urban areas should not mean building on urban green spaces.*

■ **PPG7: Countryside** – useful if your allotment is in a rural area.

■ **PPG9: Nature Conservation** – outlines the need for ecological niches in urban areas - green corridors etc.

■ **PPG17: Leisure and Recreation** Companion Guide States: *Parks, recreation grounds, playing fields and allotments must not be regarded as 'previously-developed land', as defined in Annex C of PPG3. Even where land does fall within the definition of 'previously-developed', its existing and potential value for recreation and other purposes should be properly assessed before development is considered.* The duty to assess demand for allotments is also clearly set out in paragraphs 1, 2, 3, 5 and 10.

OK, so now you have the main background information needed to begin your case. You should know the strengths and weaknesses of your case, and have done the background research to form a really good argument. Even if you find there are many things your case lacks, don't be disheartened - as long as you are aware of the issues, unless you have left it far too late, (and even then), there should always be something you can do. What you need now is a good campaign.

Campaign

We need to convince councils and Local Planning Authorities (LPAs) with reasonable argument that whilst we understand that they are short of funds and often have housing quotas to fulfil, it is as important to invest in the long term as in the short term. Well-supported allotment provision is a crucial local service, which we have the right to expect. Councils should be working for us, however cash strapped they are.

Happy communities save money in the long term because they cut crime levels and promote mental and physical health and wellbeing. A well put together campaign should highlight this, and make councils feel good about providing such a cheap and important service.

Planning decisions
Armed with your background information on the local plans and planning policy, the next step is to check out what is being planned for the site by going to the local council planning office and looking at the plans. This will give you extra information around which to base your campaign. It will also be useful to compare what is being planned by looking at the Local Development Framework and development policies to find out if the housing quota is being filled for example, or what the LDF says about development in relation to that particular area.

If the LPA is pushing for the development, you should consider in the first instance whether your campaign could get this submission taken away from the local authority and put to Public Inquiry (see *Public Inquiry* towards the end of this chapter).

If nothing has yet been planned for the site, your job at present will be easier. You can work on gaining public support for your campaign (see *Make Friends!* below). If planning applications have been submitted and one has been provisionally accepted, you will also want to find out the date of the council planning meeting to accept or reject the planning application, so you know how much time you have for your campaign. This will not be very long – two months or so.

Material considerations

Rejection of planning applications is based on what are called material considerations, which are clear objections related to land use. This is the way the land is used now, the way the land will be used if the development goes ahead, the way the development will restrict future use of the land, or the way the land could be used if the development does not go ahead.

It's no good objecting to a sell-off simply because you and your neighbours don't want it. Your material considerations need to be clear and rational. Sit down, have a cup of tea and try to get yourself into that impartial Government Planning Officer mindset.

It must be noted here though, that any objection which emphasises the effect on the community or the amenity of the area can act as a material consideration. This has worked in the past for genuine heartfelt considerations, and drops in property prices, neither material considerations in themselves, but barometers of the effect on the community of the loss of the land. Bear this in mind, but don't concentrate on making a case entirely from non-material considerations.

The material considerations you will be taking into account to be most effective will not only be against the development itself, but also can be strongly based around Agenda 21 tenets – sustainability and social economy. You can then ask yourself a series of questions around this to get an idea of how to direct your campaign:

- What is being planned for the site? A new school? Social housing? Luxury flats?
- Who is the site being sold to? Self-interested business? Charity?
- What alternatives are being offered if this site goes – are they satisfactory?
- Are there other satisfactory areas of open space in the area?
- What does the community gain from the site? What could the community gain?
- How will the local neighbourhood be affected by the proposed development?
- Will it contribute to noise/pollution/traffic in the area?

- Is there any rare wildlife on the site?
- Are there any trees with Tree Preservation Orders (TPO) on the site?
- Is the site of any historical interest? (local history/archaeology groups can be useful here)
- Put together your own ideas for the site highlighting the positive alternative uses and community support for your campaign, emphasising health, environment, and food poverty issues

There are other considerations you could take into account, including spoiling the view from a local beauty spot, for example. Your material considerations could also include specific allotments campaigning:

- Has the site been properly publicised or let out to tenants?
- Has it been properly maintained?
- Has an adequate alternative site been offered?

If you can, try to persuade your local authority or individual allotment associations to make public the number of people on allotment waiting lists, or the number of inquiries that they have received. You can also try to find out - for example, by ringing the council or checking committee reports in the library - what publicity efforts have been made to fill allotment vacancies and how easy it is to apply for them. Quote the relevant parts of the Government's Select Committee Report on the Future of Allotments, and the Government's Response to it.

St Stephen's Allotment Society won on heritage grounds, and the fact that Bath depends upon green corridors. Vic Finlayson says: "We had an architectural expert who demolished the housing plans. Beaufort Homes, the developers, were pathetic when it came to a stand-up fight. The planning application was rejected on the grounds that this green part of Lansdown has to be preserved for all time. The case the developers had put forward was deeply flawed; they were proposing housing that had no part in a heritage city like Bath. If your allotment is under threat, look at all of these things – am I in a conservation area and, if not, why not?"

Working with your Local Agenda 21 Officer, find out whether the council has a strategy for nature conservation or biodiversity. You could also use sustainability principles (see Local Authorities and Sustainability in Chapter 5, Reinvention) which the council will have signed up to as part of your campaign. Combine this with the council Core Values and/or their Best Value commitments, highlighting how this development will fall short of these commitments.

Sustainability issues in themselves do not as yet count as material considerations within the planning system. As sustainability becomes more of a central issue in local and national policy, this will change. It must also be noted that new LDF legislation has a strong commitment to sustainability built in, and relevant PPG/PPS can also be referred to. Sustainability issues can be used effectively in any public campaign and count as a material consideration due to their impact on the community amenity. The term 'sustainability' is often taken out of context – so make sure you are referring to environmental sustainability (rather than economic, for example).

Planning proposals and change of use for your site occasionally qualify for an Environmental Impact Assessment (EIA). This is particularly the case if the development is described as a Schedule 2 development, which would be for most industrial uses and major urban development (e.g. housing schemes over 1000 units, or developments over 5 hectares). Follow this up with your LPA and lobby the Secretary of State if the EIA is not carried out.

You may also want to meet with the Planning Officer assigned to the application to find out more about the application and the council's response to it. This person will be responsible for writing the report advising the Planning Committee whether or not to accept the application. Don't try to lobby this person, just find out the facts to give you a better understanding of the case.

Campaigning tactics
Whatever the status of your site, try to campaign positively and involve the local community. Don't get caught up in political and personal arguments with the site landlords. You can also be branded as a

'troublemaker' and ignored, or be seen as a threat. Such arguing wastes time, could destroy your reputation, and gets you uselessly angry.

Some general tips:

- Don't be antagonistic with anybody. No one listens to anger. Even to unreasonable people, maintaining courteous and dignified behaviour keeps you feeling strong.
- Talk to a lot of people and take any opportunity to network.
- Make links with people who have had the same experience.
- Do a lot of careful listening, even if you disagree.
- Check all the information you are given. Just because someone in authority tells you something doesn't mean it is correct.
- Take stock on a regular basis. Thinking time is very important – it is all too easy to run around like a headless chicken and miss golden opportunities.
- Accept that not everyone is on your side – whatever they may say.
- Use events (parties and social occasions) to boost morale.
- Dig in for a long fight; don't go away; don't give up.

Work in a team

Groups tend to carry more weight than individuals. Chris Carver says: "Get a community group formed, so the people campaigning are not just allotment holders, otherwise people think it's out of fashion, a few old men, and it doesn't matter. Friends of the Earth were involved for a long time. We also formed an allotment association to save the site, and a community group was formed from the public on the issue, so 1,500 people were involved as well as the allotment holders. We got 150 people to a public meeting, because over the years lots of them had had allotments."

If an allotment association is involved which you are not yet part of, present them with the issues involved, and the information you have gathered so that they can become part of the campaign.

Within a group, you might want to split tasks according to who's best suited to what. Keep in good contact with each other so you know what everyone's doing and you don't repeat yourselves or make mistakes. You might also want to rotate responsibilities. Support each other and be ready to step in to another role if someone else is having trouble and asks for help. (See Chapter 3, *Organisation*, for more details on group working).

Make friends!

Contact other local groups who may also be against planning permission – age well or youth groups, and wildlife groups, for example. They may not be directly into vegetable growing, but may want to preserve the open space for other reasons. If the planning permission isn't too far advanced, you could begin a project or interest an existing group into starting a project on the site, which could gain more support for your case.

Vic Finlayson from St Stephen's again: "We had many experts on our side - including the Bath Preservation Society, and the Georgian Society. We built up a broad front of defenders – as broad as we could, including the police (by pointing out how it would affect traffic flow within local schools), councillors, and the local and national press and television. We even got UNESCO on our side, because Bath is a heritage city." All these people sent letters of support, including the police, which worked wonders!

It's not just experts who can be useful – anyone high profile can help you with your case. Cultivate them. Good publicity helps with this, and then the big names help create even bigger publicity.

Publicity

At this point, armed with all the information, you can take your campaign to the wider community. You will also want to keep in mind ways of mobilising latent community support and action. Start a letter-writing and a poster/leaflet campaign highlighting the issues involved, and the harm any development would cause. Some aspects your campaign could include:

- Highlight positive allotment issues such as healthy, clean food, and exercise.
- What the loss of green space would mean for the community in terms of mental and physical health.

- Draw attention to the council's and government's commitment to community and the environment. If you can find something in the council's core values, then so much the better.
- If none exists, or the existing one is inadequate, draft an alternative council policy protecting and promoting allotments and green open space, and publicise this, maybe including a supporting petition.
- Provide information for action – addresses to write to with objection
- Make a ready-made letter of objection for people to sign and to send to the planning department.
- Set a date and venue for a public meeting.
- Start up a local group specifically working against the sell-off and development plans.
- Plan an event – a social or demonstration.

Get hold of the telephone number that people need to ring to rent an allotment, and publicise it. Find out how many people in the area actually want allotments and didn't know how to get one, and build this into your campaign.

Community consultation

The Government has highlighted and supported wide community consultation when the sell-off of sites is involved. In conjunction with your LA21 officer you could put together a 'community consultation' or an 'allotments assessment' exercise around the site asking people what they'd like to see the site used for if it's to remain as open space. These community planning exercises are run through partnerships between community groups and Agenda 21 departments in inner city areas earmarked for new development. They are interactive, involving maps and models of the site now and with possible futures which can be modified or commented on. You could work with your local college to make this exercise cheap and full of 'experts'.

Make sure you build any positive outcome of the consultation into your campaign.

Working with the media

Contact the press with your story. This could be either specialist gardening journals or local or national press, local TV and radio. Good media coverage can be a cornerstone in any successful campaign or campaigning event, gaining you support and vital publicity. You could invite the press to your public meeting, for example. Any national lobby group will have experience with dealing with the media and can help you with your campaign – often, there's no point in staging an event if it is not sufficiently covered in the media.

Press releases

The way to alert the media to your issue is to write a brief, one-page press release detailing the central issues involved. Press releases use a standard format as follows:

- It will need to be on headed paper from your group or a community group you are working with.
- Write 'PRESS RELEASE' at the top.
- Use a typewriter or a word processor with a clear typeface.
- Give it an eye-catching title, 'HUNDRED YEAR OLD GRANDMOTHER BATTLING TO KEEP HER PLOT', kind of thing. Your title should be typed in capitals, in bold, about three lines above the text.
- At the top right hand corner, include the date from which your release can be made public, so the journalists know when their news will be old news.
- If you want it reported upon now, write 'immediate release' top left, in line with your date.
- If it is built around the event you want covered, or you don't want the news made public until a specific date write 'embargoed until date', again, top left.
- The line spacing should be one and a half or double-spaced.
- Keep it short and to the point without overlong paragraphs – journalists have short attention spans.
- Try to include a quote from someone in a position of responsibility (the more well-known the better).
- When it is finished, type 'ENDS'.
- Include, 'for further information please contact' with names and

contact details – telephone number and possibly e-mail. If you place this information before 'ENDS', expect it to be included in the article. Always include two contacts with day and evening telephone numbers.

- You could build the release around a specific event or meeting, so journalists can get a grip on something.
- If you want photographs in the media of your event, include details of a photo call after 'ENDS', with 'Photo call' following this with the date, place, and time for it, and what will be happening. Less formally, if the event will simply produce some nice photos, just write 'Photo opportunities'.

Press releases are very important. A good example of a release is in the appendix. Remember to proofread it manually – spell checkers don't cover everything.

Get the names of the relevant journalist, editor or broadcaster to target; it could be the environment correspondent, or the news editor, with their direct fax number or e-mail address, by calling the relevant newspaper. Then fax away! Follow up your press release with telephone calls to the relevant journalist so you don't get forgotten. The more you badger them, the more likely you are to get noticed. Try to walk that fine line between being completely irritating and in your face and maintaining a high, interesting profile. Choose the most charismatic person of your group for this job!

Cultivate your journalist

Different journalists like different things, it all depends upon what kind of show, or newspaper you are sending to, but they're all always after interesting copy – good angles. Journalists are hard-edged; if the story doesn't have a catchy angle, they won't use it. They like personal stories, and want the '5 Ws' answered – Who, Where, Why, What, and When – so bear this in mind when writing your press release.

Interviews

Journalists like a good argument – anticipate difficult questions and prepare yourself before any interview. They are after good 'sound bites', and a bit of humour always goes down well. If you find anything particularly difficult, or don't feel prepared, you can always get a list of questions and ask them to ring back later. Be reasonable, talk their language, and don't alienate them. Often journalists will want to keep in touch with you to find out of any developments – cultivate them.

Journalists sometimes get things wrong. Make sure you spell out what you want them to say. Be careful about what you say, and make sure that if you do say something you don't want printed, they are aware that it is off the record (but try not to do this at all if you can help it). If they still misquote you, get in touch and say why you were upset with a story, or write to the letters page.

It is worth being aware of worst-case scenarios with the media. Gerard Lordahl, of The Neighbourhood Open Space Coalition, one of several groups campaigning to save the community gardens in New York offers the following advice: "Be careful with the media, they often pitted housing needs against the gardens and the press was more damaging than helpful. Know your facts and prove false statements." (That said, their campaign 'There Oughta be a Law' was strong enough to attract celebrities like Bette Midler, who helped to rescue over 50 gardens by buying them from the City for $2.5m).

Don't let possible bad press get you down; all publicity is good publicity. As Oscar Wilde said: "There's only one thing in the world worse than being talked about, and that's not being talked about." You're there to stir up issues and get people thinking and talking.

Never answer a point that you do not know the answer to. Simply say that you will get back to them on that point. Find out the answer and ring them back even if it is after the story has been published. This increases your media credibility - they will come back to you rather than the developer.

Check George Monbiot's *Activist's Guide to the Media* on The Land Is Ours website, or the *Sceptical Campaigner's Guide for Dealing with the Media*, from the Seeds for Change website, for more information.

Extra angles
Some of the objections you discovered when you looked into the material considerations may not be relevant in planning law, but may be very useful to gain support and attract the media. This includes personal angles, individual's hypocrisy (a very rich person trying to sell an allotment site, spending millions on his own garden), and background information on dodgy dealings. Use your common sense about what you actually put into a press release and what piece of juicy information you might just 'let slip' quietly, off the record, at some other time, for the journalist to follow up.

Don't base your campaign around such things, because statements about the individual's/company's private designs and interests are not taken into account by the planners, and could ruin your reputation. Remember to be very careful what you say – powerful individuals and companies have been known to use libel laws as a means of silencing activists. If you are worried, take legal advice.

Formal objections
Publicity combined with a good argument against development should produce a rash of well-argued letters and petitions to the planning department. These will all be taken into account when the final decision comes to be made. Keep an eye out for the date of that decision and publicise that date to get your letters in on time. The more letters sent in, from as many community groups, concerned organisations and members of the public, the better, as this will show the council how important the site is to people. Include the address given and the reference number of the planning application on all correspondence.

Petitions are counted as a single objection, so they are often more trouble than they are worth. If you can't get people to write individual letters, circulate a standard single sheet letter. These should be laid out with the core argument with dotted lines for the objector to put their address, date and signature. People are lazy and unless it can be helped, don't leave them with the letter but after they have signed it take it from them, place them in individual envelopes and hand deliver to the planning office. This takes little more time than a petition but each one submitted counts as an objection. Always have a final line requesting that the LPA keep the person informed of progress on the application.

Your letters should include all the material considerations including PPG and Local Plan/Local Development Framework violation, if applicable, to the planning department of your local council. These will be taken into account once the planning decision comes to be made. Try also to include positive uses for the site if planning permission is refused, and how the site is or could be turned into a vibrant open space.

These letters and petitions should be directed to the Secretary of State if the issue is one of the council applying to have a statutory site taken out of allotment status. This is especially important if the council appears to have been deliberately running down your site, or not effectively promoting it.

Planning Committee

It is a good idea to attend a couple of meetings of the Planning Committee in advance to see how the meetings work. Take note of how individual councillors vote in order to see who might support you. Talk to them and ask them for their advice. Through prudent contact with people you could get positive support.

Lobby your local councillors with your objections and evidence of community support. This will also be very useful once in the Planning Committee meeting, as members of the public are not always able to speak but councillors can. Many of them will back you and help you for their own political reasons. Someone may be friendly with your local councillor, or he/she may have an allotment plot – so much the better! You may also find that opposing political parties with potential councillors will support you for future election prospects.

A big word of caution should be added in relation to too much
lobbying: Planning Committee members must enter the meeting
with an open mind. They cannot do that if they have already
expressed a view and therefore too much pressure could result in a
sympathetic councillor not being able to vote.

Rules vary between local authorities about 'public access slots' in
council meetings – check with your council. Most councils allow
limited speaking by objectors and supporters, usually about three
minutes. This is though changing as many authorities are now
moving over to smaller area committees. In this case you will get
about five minutes to speak.

If you decide to address your local Planning Committee, some
campaigners advise that you dress appropriately (i.e. similarly to the
people you are addressing). Be clear about what you want to say and
make sure that you stick to their time restriction. Don't over-run
and then find you are out if time before the main point.

Chris Maile, of the Campaign for Planning Sanity says: 'My own
tactic in applications is not to lobby planning councillors, but a day
or two before the committee meet, circulate to all members a bullet-
pointed list, never more than a page and a half (councillors get reams
of papers to read). With only three minutes you get virtually nothing
said and therefore you can refer to the paper and speak to it, and
thus if you cannot get through it all you know they have something.'

Keep in touch with the council for the date of the decision. You could also
inform the media of the date so whatever the outcome, it is newsworthy.

If the planning application is refused, the developer is entitled to
appeal against it. In this case there is still lots to do to prepare for the
appeal, but you stand a better chance at this stage. If it is thrown out
of appeal, the developer could put in another application later.

Ian Goodbrand from Telferton Allotments explains: 'Every two years
Betts can put in a reshuffle plan. With planning permission for
houses it's worth £7 million - it's a four-acre site – but without

planning permission, it's classed as marginal land and worth £140,000... Investigations are being made by the council into other options such as compulsory purchase or zoning. It's an ongoing campaign until we can purchase the land.'

With the introduction of the new Planning Act, LPAs will now have the power to refuse any application that is pending either for a decision of the Secretary of State or an Inquiry, or where one of a similar nature has been refused for the last two years. This power is discretionary, so lobby your authority to use it!

Public Inquiry

Before tackling your LPA directly at Planning Committee, campaigns should always consider whether it would be worthwhile getting the development taken away from the LPA and put to a Public Inquiry. Often this is the only way forward for LPAs which are pushing the development. This can be very productive if it is targeted well.

Appeals against planning applications can be made before or after planning permission has been decided, if it can be argued that the development is of more than local importance, or that it is contrary to local plan policy, or if the developer appeals against the refusal of a planning application. It is rare for the Secretary of State to call in an application, as there is a reluctance to intervene in local political decisions, but it is a possibility.

In most cases you would start with a letter to the Secretary of State at the Regional Government Office, you then respond against with in depth grounds for calling to Inquiry. Finally, target your local MP and others in authority to back your request.

In the first instance, application to the Secretary of State would go to a Planning Inquiry. This takes one of three forms – **Written Representation**, where the Inspector will base their decision on written submissions only; an **Informal Hearing**, which takes the form of a round table discussion; or a formal **Public Inquiry**. Of these, only the Public Inquiry is adversarial: that is to say, the various sides are able to employ advocates to guide the presentation of their cases and to cross-examine witnesses. All Public Inquiries are held in the presence of an Inspector from the Planning Inspectorate who makes the final decisions on the issues involved: it may take weeks or even months for decisions to be published. All Inquiries are public, and anyone is allowed in to watch and listen to proceedings.

If you originally objected to the Planning Application, you will be informed if an Inquiry is called; you will have the right to submit evidence in writing. Your right to appear in person is at the discretion of the Inspector. It is not normally refused. An alternative route is to apply for Rule 6 Party status (from Rule 6.6 of the Inquiry Procedure Rules) which will give you much greater rights and influence on proceedings, along with more access to information to put together a strong case. However, a Public Inquiry can be a daunting experience: big developers can afford to employ experienced barristers (even QCs!) to try and pull your case to pieces.

If you are to give evidence to an Inquiry, make sure you understand your case, and know how you will present it. If you are giving evidence at a Planning Inquiry, you may find yourself being cross-examined by a barrister, so you will need to fully understand the basis of your case and to keep a cool head. A good way to prepare is to go through a mock cross-examination, and allow someone to try and pull your arguments to pieces: this will help to identify the weaknesses in your case.

It is a good idea to get together with all the other objectors (this may include the LPA, who will have experience of other inquiries) to discuss your tactics and approach. You do not have to employ an advocate, but you will find it helpful unless you are confident about your ability to cross-examine other witnesses; the advocate does not need to be a barrister. If you do use an advocate, then it is best to arrange to share them with other objectors: this not only ensures a coherent case, but splits the cost. Remember, there is no financial assistance for objectors, and you will have to raise all the money you need to fight your case.

A final important point: Public Inquiries are not courts of law, no matter how the advocates behave. Inspectors are concerned that all relevant points are brought out and are not necessarily impressed by a barrister's flashy wordplay. They will make allowances for inexperience, and you should ask them to explain or clarify anything which you do not understand.

This is only a brief outline of what to do and expect in trying to block planning permission. As suggested in the previous chapter, it would be very useful to get more details on all of these procedures. As planning law has now been overhauled, use the contacts list for more support, and keep your eyes out for new publications.

Legal Aid

Legal fees can easily run into thousands of pounds, but don't be put off by this. There are some solicitors and barristers who will represent you for nothing, or a very low fee – particularly if you work with young legal people fresh from college. Alternatively, there are organisations willing to provide free or cheap legal advice (check Contacts List). If you need to raise money for legal advice, a good campaign will provide the basis from which to do this, like the St Stephen's Allotment Society in Bath. You're particularly lucky if you live in a rich area, of course, for people digging deep in response to a heartfelt appeal.

Alternatively, if you are very poor, contact the Legal Services Commission – you need a solicitor to make the case for you. You will usually need to be on benefits, but you can get your fees covered by this, check with individual solicitors that they are part of the Community Legal Service. Some household insurance policies and mortgage protection plans have a clause to pay for challenges that affect the value of your home. Insurance against losing, again, would only be available for court cases (contact the Campaign for Planning Sanity for more details).

If the worst happens

If the planning application is accepted, you as a local citizen will not be able to appeal against it (unless you managed to get it called in to Inquiry - see above).

Another option of last resort is Judicial Review through the High Court if the council has taken a really outrageous decision - which no reasonable person could have arrived at. Applications must be made promptly - within six weeks if the appeal has already gone to

Inquiry, or three months; if three months has been exceeded, an application for an extension time should be submitted. High Court matters can be extremely expensive and you should talk to a competent solicitor before doing anything like this.

Otherwise, that's pretty much that. The only form of protest open to you now is direct action (go to *Direct Action* section below), or you could go on holiday and come back refreshed and ready to get involved in something new (see *Look after Yourself*, below). A higher body, such as a government department may be able to intervene and hold an inquiry at this stage.

Non-violent direct action

The phrase 'direct action' can make some people feel uncomfortable. This is, in part, the reaction to the tree protestors in the 1990s who loudly and peacefully drew attention to road building in Britain. However, direct action is not simply about tree protesting, and it is not necessarily illegal. Direct action can be described as any action you take as an individual to assert your views on issues you see as important. It can be as simple as not buying a particular brand, because the company has a poor human rights record, or choosing where to shop – for example, shopping locally to keep the local economy alive.

Non-violent direct action is a very important part of the political process and has been used to highlight important issues for hundreds of years. The suffragettes were direct activists, as was Mahatma Gandhi, the Greenpeace protestors on Piper Alpha, against oil pollution, or the recent GM activists pulling up experimental crops.

There are two types of direct action – the first, protesting against what you see to be unlawful action on the part of developers which you may want to use while the campaign is going on. Allotment holders whose site is under threat frequently take direct action when ignoring eviction notices and continuing to cultivate the soil. They are simply voting with their feet (and their spades), ignoring their landlord's directions. If your site is centrally important to you, then a direct action to prevent or draw attention to the bulldozers coming in is a risk you might want to take. Also, if you can create wider support and uproar, you can be invaluable in helping to highlight important issues everywhere.

Another type of direct action could be used after the planning decision has been made. Some campaigners feel that direct action can work for them if they have pursued all other avenues open and still feel that the local planning system and council have not given them a fair hearing. They may want to use direct action to show developers and officials how important the site is to them and how unpopular the development is to the local community, or to highlight what they see as issues of national importance. Bear in mind that you will lose credibility as a campaigner if you have not at least tried to fight the application through the official channels first.

There are many different things you can do. It is perfectly legal and very inclusive to stage a demonstration outside the site, with banners and your petition. If you choose to demonstrate, inform the local police of your intentions, and make a day of it. However, people undertaking non-violent direct action have done many other things – not always strictly legal, but always respectful of human life. Roads protestors have built tree houses, tunnels, and chained themselves in, Greenpeace have sailed small boats in front of whaling ships to prevent whaling. The suffragettes chained themselves to railings. Gandhi sat.

The community gardeners in New York City used direct action in February 2000 as part of their campaign to save their sites. Gerard Lordahl of The Neighbourhood Open Space Coalition describes their tactics: 'Dozens of community gardeners chained themselves to cement blocks that they had buried in the garden months before, to prepare for the time when the police and bulldozers would arrive. They also constructed a bulldozer blockade to prevent the destruction of a particular garden on East 7th Street in Manhattan wedged between two apartment buildings.

'This encampment was also equipped with lockdown boxes, elevated sitting tripods and other civil disobedience devices including a huge frog on stilts over the garden gate large enough to house three protestors. In Puerto Rican legend the frog or coqui is said to be a talisman that repels attackers and is revered for its huge voice despite its small size. It took several policemen on ladders to remove the protestors from the coqui.'

Non-violent direct action can and should be safe and fun, and the media love it. Make sure it draws attention to the positive issues around the site, and shows the support and demand for the site. Issue a statement to this effect – you can use all the petitions and letters you used in your campaign. Try to involve your local community and don't import a whole load of seasoned direct activists – it needs to be your action, something you want to do to draw attention to your cause, and also the national issues involved.

It is vitally important that you build a strong media campaign around anything you do – it will be wasted otherwise. The media will love any picture they can find of a local Swampy locked on to a shed with 85-year-old Bob who's been gardening for 60 years etc. This also applies to the national media, who love allotments but often cannot find anything interesting to make a story around. The more original the campaign you have organised, the better. Think of it as a non-confrontational sit-in. The driving force behind your action, however, should always be the protection of the environment, or your right to garden - not a publicity event.

If your planned direct action involves breaking the law, make sure that the action is preceded by a legal briefing for those involved to ensure that people know and understand the risks of arrest, and the potential consequences (contact Seeds for Change for info). One of you should be given the job of legal observer to record the details of those arrested, what they were doing, numbers of police officers, and so on, and then to arrange solicitors and bail. This person must not be involved in any other way in the action – but they should be armed with cameras, paper and a mobile phone.

Make sure that people who are going to take part in the direct action are careful that they don't drag other people in with them who don't want to be involved. Do it in your own name, or create a new group specifically for the action. Don't do it in the name of people who don't want to be involved or legally implicated in it. As Alan Rees, the current Chair of the National Society of Allotment and Leisure Gardeners has said: "Personally, I have stood in front of a

JCB, but the National Society could not be seen to do something illegal.' (*The Guardian*, 26/04/00)

Similarly, it is important that if you don't want to be involved in the action, but want to provide public support, make sure you provide that support after the event has begun rather than before, so you can't be linked if you don't want to be.

Look after yourself

You are important! Nobody but the most dedicated with many resources at their disposal can run a successful continuous campaign. If you lose your case, which you might – don't give up – it's such a waste to see dedicated, original, idealistic people dejected over the loss of a site. As a community activist you are a vitally important part of your community, but you are useless if you are burnt out.

Take some time out for yourself. Any battle is draining and campaigners have a shelf life. Start again with the experience you've gained. Maybe you will choose not to take a central part in another battle again, but support others. You might decide to put your energies into a positive and reviving project which shows how strong communities can be. Whatever you do, try to live sustainably – nurturing yourself, as well as your allotment and the world around you.

We are moving towards a greener future, and will one day regret the loss of our special urban open space. You and your community will become heroes for having fought in the struggle.

The last word is best left to Vic Finlayson:

On the day we won, we planted a rose on the wall called 'New Dawn' with a tablet reading, 'On this day, these allotments were saved from the bulldozer'. Any time you come to Bath, you can see the rose blooming on the wall.

Contacts

This booklet only contains a drop in the ocean of the enormous amount of info out there. This list is another drop in that ocean; if each contact has a similar list, the information and contacts could widen exponentially. Enjoy!

Allotments Groups, Community Groups, Activists and Interesting Individuals

ALLOTMENTS AND VEGETABLE GARDENING RING – WEBSITE

This website provides links to many of the the major (and minor!) allotment sites in the UK and beyond. A very good place to start tapping into the wealth of web-based allotment and community garden information out there.

e: allotments@dial.pipex.com
w: http://q.webring.com/hub?ring=allotmentring

AVON ORGANIC GROUP

54 Castlegate House, School Road, Bristol BS4 4ND

A flourishing Bristol-based group which organises talks, discussions, visits, workdays and a seed swap. They produce a newsletter and sell literature, organic goods and informally network groups in the city. They also have a stall at Bristol Farmers' Market in summer and autumn. Some members run a community orchard on an allotment site.

e: avonorganicgroup@onetel.com
w: www.beehive.thisisbristol.co.uk/avonorganics

SIMON BADDELEY

34 Beaudesert Road, Handsworth, Birmingham B20 3TG

Local campaigner for parks, allotments and green spaces in Handsworth. Convener of Handsworth Allotments Information Group (HAIG) fighting to save privately-owned Victoria Jubilee Allotments. Knowledgeable in community politics, especially land use. National/international networker; internet regular.

t: 0121 554 9794   **m:** 07775 655842.
e: s.j.baddeley@bham.ac.uk

BARMPTON LANE ALLOTMENT ASSOCIATION
29 Beech Road, Darlington, Co Durham DL1 3HQ
Constituted in 2003, this association have already applied successfully for a grant to clear plots and planted 200 Christmas trees to raise funds. The site includes two schools plots and an plot for the 'Black Poplar Group' who have begun an endangered tree plantation.
Michael Haw, Association Chair
t: 01325 466 484

BATH ORGANIC GROUP
28 Ashley Avenue, Bath BA1 3DS
Have converted 10 disused allotments (rent-free) into an organic kitchen garden, complete with tree bog and orchard area.
Peter Andrews (chair)
t: 01225 484 472   **w:** www.bathorganicgroup.org.uk

BARRY WATSON
44 Gale Street, Dagenham, Essex RM9 4NH
Barry is the master of recycling and soil reclamation, amongst other things. Currently coordinating the Forest Farm Community Garden in Hainalt, his contacts network and information base is extensive, and often esoteric. He works with schools, therapeautic gardening, inexperienced gardeners, and refugees. Expert on compost toilets including disabled access. Experienced, informative, empowering.
t: 020 8592 8941   **e:** asmw22@dsl.pipex.com

BEANSTALK ALLOTMENTS REGENERATION PROJECT
The Centre for Environmental Initiatives, The Old School House, Mill Lane, Carshalton, Surrey SM5 2JY
Run through the Carshalton based charity, The Centre for Environmental Initiatives. Beanstalk produces a newsletter, information pack, talks and workshops for schools, community, and children's groups. They network local organic allotment groups, and have a free tool and seeds loan service. They work with the London Borough of Sutton to provide free allotments and regeneration workshops.
Simon Honey
t: 020 8770 6611   **e:** simon@thecei.org.uk

BLOOMFIELD COMMUNITY ORCHARD
19 Maple Grove, Bath BA2 3AF
Good example of a community orchard – trees, pond, willow sculpture, picnics, working parties.
Peter Andrews
t: 01225 484 472 **e:** peter@eco-logicbooks.com

BOLTON WILDLIFE PROJECT
125 Blackburn Road, Bolton B21 8HF
Involved in everything from community composting and box schemes to training courses, seed banks, contaminated soil remediation, and group networking. They have just begun a Social Prescription Scheme – linking the Health Service to allotment gardening. They just keep growing.
Kim Patterson
t: 01204 361 847 **e:** kpatterson@lancswtbolton.cix.co.uk

BOLTON GATHERING OF ORGANIC GROWERS
The Green House, 2 Northwood Cresc, Deane, Bolton BL5 3DS
A community co-operative founded in 1999 to network and promote the activities of local groups. It aims to empower people to develop 'bottom up' sustainable and co-operative solutions to problems of urban decay. Programmes include Community Gardens, Wholefood Co-operative, a crèche, and gardening and cookery courses. GOG activists have planning and legal knowlege, plus understanding and experience of community organisation. Very useful contact(s).
t: (evenings) Richard, Chair 01204 435816
t: (day) Alan, Treasurer 01204 907714
e: Kath, Secretary kathrynbaron@msn.com
w: http://bolton-organics.org.uk

BRADFORD COMMUNITY ENVIRONMENTAL PROJECT (BCEP)
Unit 13, Carlisle Business Centre, Carlisle Road, Bradford BD8 8BD
Provides support for allotment associations starting up, and helps develop community gardens and allotments. BCEP can assist with training for new allotment gardeners and holds an annual community

composting awareness event. Previously BCEP helped set up resource centres of recyclables for use on allotments and can advise on present resources. In 1999, in partnership with the local Health Authority, it ran the award winning allotment project 'Gardening for Health' which has evolved into the 'Sho Nirbhor' (Self Reliance) programme working with the Bangladeshi community. Contact former members of the Allotment Action Group through BCEP.

Jane Robinson (Sustainable Futures Team Leader)
t: 01274 223236   **e:** info@bcep.org.uk

ANNE BRADLEY
Local campaigner. Saved Old Marston Hill, Oxford, in 1997, with a huge community campaign and support. Knowledgeable in community organizing and planning.
e: AnnBradly@aol.com

BRIGHTON & HOVE ALLOTMENT FEDERATION
7 Withdean Court Avenue, Brighton, East Sussex BN1 6YF
John's areas of expertise are council allotment strategies, association leases and management agreements with councils, and successful campaigns for allotments under threat. Gave evidence on behalf of the South East to the 'Future of Allotments' parliamentary committee. The Federation have just completed three separate areas within existing sites in Brighton & Hove for 'Gardeners with Disabilities' facilities included Compostable Toilets. They are happy to share information on planning, fund raising and construction, and welcome visitors.
John Smyth (Secretary)
t: 01273 508195   **e:** allotmentfedbtnhove@ntlworld.com

CHRIS CARVER
6 Addington Close, Devizes, Wiltshire SN10 5BE
Friends of the Earth campaigner who won the first stage of her campaign to save the Spitalcroft Allotments in Devizes, with originality and sound research. Using the 'Future of Allotments' report, she suggested a policy for inclusion in the Kennet 2004 Local Plan which resulted in the inclusion of policy TR20 particularly to protect allotments and land formerly used as allotments.
t: 01380 725082   **e:** carver5@tiscali.co.uk

COLLIER ROAD ALLOTMENT ASSOCIATION, AND HASTINGS & ST LEONARD'S ALLOTMENTS FEDERATION

3 West View, Halton, Hastings, East Sussex TN34 3NZ
Keen to encourage public access to land by publicising allotments.
Special interest/expertise – gardening, allotments and health. The
Federation is keen to get everyone growing (organically) on
allotments, has had input with the health authority
planning community allotments.
Shelagh Wilson
t: 01424 713792   **e:** shelagh@wilsonm1.freeserve.co.uk

PROFESSOR DAVID CROUCH

Tourism School, Derby University, Kedleston Road Campus, Derby DE22 1GB
Allotments academic – co-authored The Allotment with Colin Ward,
now in its fourth edition. Very interested and involved in research
into community gardening and allotments. Also interested in
smallholdings; has good European contacts.
t: 01332 622222   **e:** d.c.crouch@derby.ac.uk

ECOWORKS

61b Mansfield Road, Nottingham NG1 3FN
Began 1992, this project is committed to the permaculture principles
'earth care, people care'. The Ecoworks Garden Project has been
going since 1994 from the eight plots on the Hungerhill allotment
site. It involves volunteers who both have and have not had a history
of using mental health services without making a distinction between
the two. Since 2003 it has gone down the social economy route on
an adajacent plot offering training to young people and adults and
growing and selling chemical free produce to the local market.
Paul Paine/Adrian Horsely
t: 0115 911 2522   **e:** ecoworks@gn.apc.org

FROGLIFE

White Lodge, London Road, Peterborough PE7 0LG
Goes large on amphibians. Works with allotment groups.
t: 01733 558844   **w:** www.froglife.org

GREATER LONDON ALLOTMENTS FORUM (GLAF)

New independent forum for networking, promoting and protecting allotments in London.

Colin Bowen, Chair

t: 0208 527 095   **m:** 07903 017844

e: colin@cdbowen.freeserve.co.uk

HIGHAM HILL COMMON ALLOTMENTS ASSOCIATION

Green Pond Road, Walthamstow, London   E17 6JB

Successful allotment community association with particular focus on community development and equality. They run an 'Allotments for All' campaign, working with voluntary and community organizations to promote a safe environment for groups who experience barriers, (including physical, policy and cultural barriers), to participating in allotment communities. They welcome support for the campaign.

Colin Bowen, Secretary

t: 0208 527 0958   **m:** 07903 017844

e: colin@cdbowen.freeserve.co.uk

website: www.actionlink.org.uk/hhcaa

LEAF (LOCAL ENTERPRISES AROUND FOOD)

Community Room, Southey Library, Moonshine Lane, Sheffield S5 8RB

Coordinates a user-led Community Allotments Project in a north Sheffield regeneration area, supporting and helping local residents and community groups to learn food growing. Well networked with other Sheffield allotment projects, and the Sheffield Women's Allotment Project. Knowedgeable on community development work and funding.

Rose, Zoy, or Lucy

t: 0114 285 4479

MOULSECOOMB FOREST GARDEN AND WILDLIFE PROJECT

Bates Estate Community Flat, 26 Selsfield Drive, Brighton BN2 4HA

Active and vibrant open access community food project situated on eight plots on the Moulsecoomb Place allotments. Programme of free events include Pond Dipping, Herb Walks, Moth Nights and Tree I.D. Regular visits from all local schools & playgroups, disabled

adults from City College, Young Offenders, excluded and special
needs kids. They are keen on seed saving and are Seed Guardians for
the HDRA; check their 'Outlawed Vegetable Garden'. Their book
Seedy Business: Tales From the Allotment Shed, is available on their
website.
Tel: 01273 707656
e-mail: info@forestgarden.fsnet.co.uk
website: www.seedybusiness.org.uk

Elder Stubbs Allotments
Rymers Lane, Oxford OX4 3LB
This site, a Charitable Trust, was founded in 1852 for the 'deserving,
labouring poor' under the Cowley Encosure Act. Once 60% derelict,
it is now a functional site with a waiting list, because it has
diversified. It has a woodland of over a thousand trees, a pond and
sculpture area, a heritage orchard with 45 varieties of old English
apple and plays host to two organizations, Restore (see below), and
Steppin' Stone, a homelessness and long term unemployment
project. The Charity has funds from investments from the sale of a
piece of its land and makes financial and practical contributions to
these projects.
John Purviss   Tel: 01865 725 051

Elder Stubbs Garden Group
Elder Stubbs Allotments, Rymers Lane, Oxford OX4 3LB
The Garden Group is part of Restore, is a community based mental
health project providing valuable work and social experience. The
Elder Stubbs part of the Restore is a flagship mental health and
foodlinks project on Elder Stubbs Allotments, Oxford. It both sells its
produce and cooks it up for lunch! It holds a very successful annual
summer event.
Roddy Chamberlain Tel: 01865 747 176

Greer Hart
30 Edgemont Street, Glasgow G41 3EL
President of the Scottish Tree Trust (began in 1982) and
representative for the Queens Park Allotments, Glasgow. Community
activist working to provide free environmental education services for
the people of Glasgow. Recycler and scavenger extraordinaire, he

has many inventive and original ideas for fundraising.
t: 0141 649 2462

HARTCLIFFE HEALTH AND ENVIRONMENT ACTION GROUP (HHEAG)

The Gatehouse Centre, Hareclive Road, Hartcliffe, Bristol BS13 9JN

An independent community based charity began in 1990 in an area of high social and health need. The area has limited access to affordable quality produce and in 1992 it began a food co-op. HHEAG has expanded into producing organic food from the local Molesworth Drive allotments, for the food co-op and a local school. HHEAG also provides formal and informal horticulture training which includes several schools that have food growing clubs or leaning as part of their curriculum. It is developing a community market garden on a disused allotment site, and aims to be a self sustaining independent enterprise in five years time.

Sue Walker
t: 0117 9465 285   **e:** sue.walker@hheag.org.uk

KITCHEN GARDENS DISCUSSION GROUP

A useful e-mail forum where new and established gardeners you can find advice and information for problems. Also discussion on allotment issues. To subscribe e-mail subscribe@yahoogroups.com

ROTHERHAM PRIMARY CARE TRUST

The Valley Allotment Project, Oak House, Moorhead Way, Bramley, Rotherham S66 1YY

Begun in 2003, this open access project, situated on the Herringthorpe Allotments in Rotherham, is a good example of local health services accessing allotments to promote health. From one hectare of previoulsy derelict allotments, it provides low cost, chemical free fruit and vegetables to a diverse, deprived local area. It involves the community in the project with the aim of becoming a sustainable commuity enterprise by 2007.

Jane Hicken
t: 01709 302 094   **e:** jane.hicken@rotherhampct.nhs

SCOTTISH ALLOTMENTS AND GARDENS SOCIETY
31 Hyndland Road, Glasgow G12 9UY
The umbrella network for allotments in Scotland. It campaigns to protect, preserve and promote allotments in Scotland. A petition from SAGS to the Scottish Parliament resulted in an inquiry by the Government Committee, published January 2003, to be followed by forthcoming Good Practice Guidelines. SAGS website provides both Scottish and English legislation, sample Consitutions, leases, funding information, information on land contamination, further links and contacts and much more. Contact SAGS for the Edinburgh and Dundee Allotment Gardens Association and the Glasgow Allotments Forum.
Judy Wilkinson
t: 0141 357 0204   **e:** secretary@sags.org.uk **w:** www.sags.org.uk

SPADEWORKS
Sturminster Road Allotments Association's project which has regenerated a 30-plot site to full occupancy, with a wildlife area. Specialities: working with the media, Association management, and fundraising.
Jean and John Mantle
t: 01275 545119

SHEFFIELD ORGANIC FOOD INITIATIVE
41b Burns Road, Sheffield, South Yorkshire S6 3GL
Runs grassroots allotment schemes, courses, a seedbank including rare and unusual varieties. Offers advice on any of the above (seedsaving a speciality) and gives talks and run workshops.
Richard Clare
t: 0114 268 6727

ST ANNE'S ALLOTMENTS PROJECT
St Anns Allotments, Unit 12, Sycamore Business Centre, Hunger Hill Road, St Annes, Nottingham NG3 4NB
75 acre site claiming to be the biggest and oldest allotment site in the world, dating back to at least 1830, with 670 plots. STAA is an organisation of allotment gardeners campaigning to protect and preserve the historic allotment site. They work with the City

Council to manage the allotments. They network with various community groups, schools and individuals who have plots.
t: 0115 911 0207   **e:** staaltd@care4free.net   **w:** www.staan.co.uk

ST STEPHEN'S ALLOTMENTS SOCIETY
Northcote, Lansdown Road, Bath BA1 5SU

Won their 5-year campaign against the Diocese of Bath and Wells to save their site from development.
Jean and Vic Finlayson
t: 01225 313072   **e:** jholmesf@waitrose.com

MARTIN STOTT
65 Divinity Road, Oxford OX4 1LH

Martin's areas of expertise are allotments and regeneration, Local Agenda 21 and local authorities. He has completed a consulation on the regeneration of an allotment site for use by a school.
e: martin.stott@talk21.com

SURREY ORGANIC GARDENING GROUP (SOGG)

Monthly meetings, guest speakers, group garden visits. They provide leaflets and information on organic gardening, and share skills. A friendly group always glad to welcome new members, whatever their experience.
Alistair Cruickshank
t: 020 8669 6692   **e:** alistair.cruickshank@blueyonder.co.uk.

TEESIDE HOMELESS ACTION
145 High Street, Redcar TS10 3DQ

Teeside Homeless Action is a user led group set up in 1997, offering help with accomodation, legal advice and meaningful activities for homeless and ex-homeless people. Their allotment project began in 1998 on three disused allotments in Saltburn. It has expanded into a community garden in Middlesbourough. Keen on organics, willow structures, polytunnels and dry stone walling.
Francis Owens
t: 01642 478 885   **e:** thag@talk21.com

TILEHURST ALLOTMENTS ASSOCIATION
85 Westwood Road, Tilehurst, Reading, Berkshire, RG31 5PY

This association transformed its site from 50% to 100% and a full waiting list within two years. Jenny Cottee also ran a successful campaign, ensured that the council put forward guidance to the trustees of its private allotment site telling them that they'd have planning permission rejected if they applied. Also secured political promises for long-term protection of the site, through their MP.

Jenny Cottee (Secretary)
t: 0118 942 5169

MICHAEL WALE
2 Clifton Avenue. Shepherd's Bush, London W12 9DR
Allotments activist, journalist and author. Can advise and help campaigners on using the media. Fought a successful campaign to save local privately owned allotments. Facilitates workshops about allotment matters sometimes with hilarious results, knowledgeable in the history of the allotment movement.
t: 020 8743 8211   **e:** michaelwale@waitrose.com

Legal

BAR PRO BONO UNIT
289-293 High Holbourn, London WC1V 7H2
Provides free legal advice and/or representation if they take on your case.
t: 020 7611 9500   **e:** enquiries@barprobono.org.uk
w: www.barprobono.org.uk

EARTHRIGHTS SOLICITORS
Springfield, Kilmington, Axminster, Devon EX13 7SB
Unique law firm committed to the defence of communities and the environment, and the promotion of the environment and stakeholder rights. Members of the Environmental Lawyers Alliance Worldwide (E-LAW). EarthRights' Charlie Hopkins has considerable knowledge of allotment law. Areas of expertise relevant to plot-holders includes eviction and village green designation. Knowledgeable on European and International law.
Charlie Hopkins
t: 01297 34405   **e:** charlie@earthrights.org.uk
w: www.earthrights.org.uk

ENVIRONMENTAL LAW FOUNDATION
Suite 309, 16 Baldwin Gardens, Hatton Square, London EC1N 7RJ

Helps individuals and community groups if they have an environmental problem. Also networks useful organisations and experts. Has Community Development Programme to provide practical advice on community regeneration issues, including land use. Provides a free initial consultation, and any further work is done at reduced cost. ELF organizes information events nationally on environmental law issues.

t: 0207 404 1030   **e:** info@elflaw.org   **w:** www.elflaw.org

PUBLIC INTEREST LAWYERS
Unit 5, Newhall Place, 16–17 Newhall Place, Birmingham B1 3JH

Public Interest Lawyers (PIL) are a team of four legal specialists providing a specialist service to individuals and groups on legal matters of public interest, including public law, human rights law, international law, environmental law and planning law. They take on some legal aid work if you qualify.

t: 0121 212 1868   **e:** info@publicinterestlawyers.co.uk
w: publicinterestlawyers.co.uk

PUBLIC LAW SOLICITORS
King Edward Chambers, 166b Alcester Road, Moseley, Birmingham B13 8HS

Specialists in public law and community care work. Public law focuses on helping individuals and organisations affected by the misuse of public powers and duties. PLS is keen to use the law to effect social change through test cases and partnerships with community groups. They are able to work nationally through telephone and e-mail and can offer reduced fees if applicable. PLS's Alastair Wallace has specialist planning knowledge and has advised community groups seeking to protect allotment sites.

t: 0121 256 0326   **e:** awallace@publiclawsolicitors.co.uk
w: www.publiclawsolicitors.co.uk

Planning

This section relates to specific planning organizations – check the whole contacts list for general contacts with planning knowledge.

CAMPAIGN FOR PLANNING SANITY

Planning Sanity helps local communities tackle adverse planning and development applications. It offers online help, an advice line, affordable training workshops, representation at public inquiries and council planning meetings, speakers for public meetings and access to a range of specialists. It offers its services at low or no cost, although donations are appreciated.
t: 0871 750 3992   **e:** info@planningsanity.co.uk
w: www.planningsanity.co.uk

PLANNING AID

National Unit, Unit 419, The Custard Factory, Gibb Street, Birmingham B9 4AA
A network of regional services providing free, independent and professional advice and support on town planning matters to community groups and individuals who cannot afford to employ a planning consultant. It aims to give people the confidence to help themselves and to become positively involved in planning issues. Contact them or check their website for your local service.
t: 0121 693 1201   **e:** info@planningaid.rtpi.org.uk
w: www.planningaid.rtpi.org.uk

THE ROYAL TOWN PLANNING INSTITUTE

41 Botolph Lane, London, EC3R 8DL
Independent charity aiming to improve the art and science of town and country planning. It seeks to secure a decent home for everyone, empower people and communities to influence decisions that affect them and improve the planning system with the principles of sustainable development.
t: 020 7929 9494   **e:** online@rtpi.org.uk
w: www.rtpi.org.uk

TOWN AND COUNTRY PLANNING ASSOCIATION
17 Carlton House Terrace, London   SW1Y 5AS
Formed in 1899, the TCPA campaigns for the reform of the UK's planning system to make it more responsive to people's needs and promote sustainable development. It includes people involved in the development industry, environmentalists, and social justice campaigners.
t: 020 7930 8903   **e:** tcpa@tcpa.org.uk   **w:** www.tcpa.org.uk

MARK JACKSON
Experience of allotment campaigning particularly on private sites. Extensive knowledge on planning, legal issues and land use – particularly relating to housing, regional planning and sustainability.
e: markjack@waitrose.com

CHAPTER SEVEN
The Potato Store, Flax Drayton Farm, South Petherton, Somerset, TA13 5LR
Chapter Seven is the Planning Office of The Land Is Ours. It campaigns for access to land for all households through environmentally-sound planning. Offers free advice on low-impact planning matters over the telephone.
Simon Fairlie
t: 01460 249204   **e:** chapter7@tlio.demon.co.uk
w: www.thelandisours.org/chapter7

Organisations

ALLOTMENTS REGENERATION INITIATIVE (ARI)
The GreenHouse, Hereford Street, Bristol, BS3 4NA
A pilot partnership project, managed by the Federation of City Farms and Community Gardens. Aims is to increase the capacity of its partner organisations to promote allotment regeneration. It is projected that ARI will be taken 'in house' by a new charity organised by the National Society of Allotment and Leisure Gardeners at the end of 2005. Supports all aspects of allotment gardening with information, training, networking and small grants.
t: 0117 963 1551   **e:** ari@farmgarden.org.uk
w: www.farmgarden.org.uk/ari

BLACK ENVIRONMENT NETWORK
1st Floor, 60 High Street, Llanberis, Wales, LL55 4EU
A networking organization which supports Black and Minority
Ethnic groups wishing to undertake environmental projects,
including allotments. Also has regional development workers who
can work alongside community groups.
t: 01286 870715   **e:** ukoffice@ben-network.org.uk
w: www.ben-network.org

ALLOTMENTS SECTION, BRISTOL CITY COUNCIL
Colston House, Colston Street, Bristol BS1 5AQ
Amongst the most forward thinking allotment offices nationally, Steve
Clampin, the Allotments Manager, supports interesting and alternative
projects on allotment sites in Bristol, as well as helping sites become
self managed. Steve can help and advise you if you need to encourage
your council's Allotment Office to new ways of thinking.
Steve Clampin
t: 0117 922 3737   **e:** steve_clampin@bristol-city.gov.uk
w: www.bristol-city.gov.uk/allotments

BTCV
**Conservation Centre, 163 Balby Road, Doncaster, S. Yorks
DH4 0RH**
Conservation body working with volunteer teams to improve the
natural environment. They offer insurance for work teams, and the
hire of equipment, and work days.
t: 01302 572 244   **e:** Information@btcv.org.uk **w:** www.btcv.org

CHARITY COMMISSION
In case you want to do some major fundraising and need charitable
status. They also offer model constitutions. Call them or check their
website for regional offices.
t: 0870 333 0123   **e:** enquiries@charitycommission.gsi.gov.uk
w: www.charitycommission.gov.uk

COMMISSION FOR RACIAL EQUALITY
201-211 Borough High Street, London SE1 1GZ
Will help address racism on your site, Contact them for your local office.
t: 020 7939 0000 **e:**   info@cre.gov.uk **w:** www.cre.gov.uk

---

COMMON GROUND

Goldhill House, 21 High Street, Shaftesbury SP7 8JE

The people who invented Apple Day. Advice on starting a community orchard and lots of examples of successful orchards on allotments. Information and wonderful ideas for events on allotments.

t: 01747 850 820   **e:** info@commonground.org
w: www.commonground.org.uk

COMMUNITY COMPOSTING NETWORK

67 Alexandra Road, Sheffield S2 3EE

Provides practical and legal information and contacts for effective community composting projects.

t: 0114 258 0483/0114 255 3720   **e:** info@communitycompost.org
w: www.communitycompost.org

FEDERATION OF CITY FARMS & COMMUNITY GARDENS (FCF&CG)

The GreenHouse, Hereford Street, Bedminster, Bristol BS3 4NA

Works to represent the views of its members to national and international bodies and raise the profile of community farming and gardening. Provides advice, information and support on all aspects of community gardening to community projects. Develops network links between projects.

t: 0117 923 1800   **e:** admin@farmgarden.org.uk
w: www.farmgarden.org.uk

GREENPEACE

Canonbury Villas, London N1 2PN

An international campaigning organisation working to defend nature and bring about environmental solutions.

t: 020 7865 8100 **e:** info@uk.greenpeace.org **w:** www.greenpeace.org.uk

FRIENDS OF THE EARTH

26-28 Underwood Street, London N1 7JQ

Environmental campaigning group working internationally, nationally and locally for a more accountable government, healthier environment, and fairer society. They run the Real Food Campaign – lobbying for safe, healthy food. They have a good planning department. Contact them for details of your local group.

t: 020 7490 1555   **e:** info@foe.co.uk   **w:** www.foe.co.uk

GROUNDWORK UK
85-87 Cornwall Street, Birmingham, B3 3BY
A federation of Trusts in England, Wales and Northern Ireland, each
working with partners to improve the quality of the local
environment, lives of local people and success of local businesses in
areas in need of investment. Supporting practical projects, in every
aspect of community work. Contact them for your local Trust.
t: 0121 236 8565   **w:** www.groundwork.org.uk

HENRY DOUBLEDAY RESEARCH ASSOCIATION (HDRA)
**National Centre for Organic Gardening, Ryton-on-
Dunsmore, Coventry CV8 3LG**
Europe's largest organic gardening organisation, HDRA offers
practical organic advice and carries out scientific research into
organic horticultural techniques. It also saves old, unusual and
outlawed seeds through its Heritage Seed Library. Has leaflets, three
display gardens and conference centre.
t: 024 7630 3517   **e:** enquiry@hdra.org.uk **w:** www.hdra.org.uk

THE LAND IS OURS
**The Potato Store, Flax Drayton Farm, South Petherton,
Somerset TA13 5LR**
Campaigns for access to land and the decision-making processes
affecting it for all regardless of age, race, gender, or disability.
Simon Fairlie
t: 01460 249204 **e:** chapter7@tlio.demon.co.uk
w: www.thelandisours.org or www.tlio.org.uk

MEDIATION UK
Alexander House, Telephone Avenue, Bristol BS1 4BS
Voluntary organisation dedicated to developing constructive means
of resolving conflicts in communities. It covers all aspects of conflict
resolution and mediation services including advice, information,
consultancy, training programmes and the development of Quality
Assurance. Contact them for your local service.
t: 0117 904 6661   **e:**enquiry@mediationuk.org.uk
w: www.mediationuk.org.uk

NATIONAL SOCIETY OF ALLOTMENT & LEISURE GARDENERS
O'Dell House, Hunters Road, Corby, Northants NN17 5JE
National representative body for the UK allotment movement. Aims to
protect allotments for future generations and campaigns for improvements to
legislation. Provides an information service including a quarterly magazine
free to members and available to non members by subscription.
Geoff Stokes, National Secretary
t: 01536 266576 **e:** natsoc@nsalg.org.uk **w:** www.nsalg.org.uk

FARMA (National Farmers' Retail and Markets Organisation)
FARMA supports local food growing and distribution. It works with all
forms of selling direct to consumers, including box schemes, farm shops,
and farmers' markets. Has a list of 250 farmers' markets (www.
farmersmarkets.net) and 500 farm shops (www.farmshopping.com). For
a shop or market near you, check the websites.
t: 0845 458 8420 **e:** justask@farma.org.uk **w:** www.farma.org.uk

VOLUNTEERING ENGLAND
New Oxford House, 16 Waterloo Street, Birmingham B2 5UG
Promotes, supports, and lobbies for volunteering. Contact them for the
address of your local volunteer bureau.
t: 0845 305 6957 **e:** information@volunteeringengland.org
w: www.navb.org.uk

NATIONAL PLAYING FIELDS ASSOCIATION (NPFA)
NPFA Fields Office, 12 Park Road, Coventry, CV1 2LD
National organisation for the protection and improvement of playing
fields and recreational space. Protects almost 2,000 sites, and owns over
150 sites. Acquires and protects land, in partnership with local
communities, and helps them set up charitable trusts to manage the land.
It can include allotments, but must include areas for community use -
recreation or playing fields for example.
Rocky Sharrock
t: 02476 222 308 **e:** fields@npfa.co.uk **w:** www.playing-fields.com

PERMACULTURE ASSOCIATION
BCM Permaculture Association, London WC1N 3XX
Networking and advice-giving association promoting permaculture.
Ahould be able to help with designs for tree bogs.
t: 0845 458 1805 **w:** www.permaculture.org.uk

PLANTS FOR A FUTURE (PFAF)

A vegan permaculture project which seeks to find unusual plants for different uses, including non-food uses, and to replace animal products. They have an extensive database of useful plants, publication information, run courses – contact them for more details.

t: 01208 873 554/01208 872 963   **w:** www.pfaf.org

SEEDS FOR CHANGE

Provides training and support to groups involved in environmental and social justice issues. Aims to share campaigning skills and experience. Free training to local groups on group faciliation including consensus decisionmaking, coping with internal politics and burnout, campaign skills, planning your campaign, working with the media, direct action.

t: 0845 330 7583 (Lancaster) 0845 458 4776 (Oxford)
e: oxford@seedsforchange.org.uk; lancaster@seedsforchange.org.uk
w: www.seedsforchange.org.uk

SOIL ASSOCIATION

Bristol House, 40-56 Victoria Street, Bristol BS1 6BY

The largest promoter and certifier of organic food in the UK. Provides information about organic food and organises training and advice for farmers. Runs a network of organic farms open to schools and the public. The Local Food Department helps organisations source local organic food.

t: 0117 314 5000   **e:** info@soilassociation.org
w: www.soilassociation.org

SUSTAIN - THE ALLIANCE FOR BETTER FOOD AND FARMING

94 White Lion Street, London N1 9PF

Campaigns for food and agriculture policies that enhance the welfare of people and animals, improving working and living environment, promoting equity and enriching society and culture. Publications include a directory of local food growing projects. Urban agriculture and healthy eating initiatives.

t: 020 7837 1228 **e:** sustain@sustainweb.org **w:** www.sustainweb.org

THRIVE

The Geoffrey Udall Centre, Beech Hill, Reading RG7 2AT

A horticultural charity that exists to enable disadvantaged, disabled and older people to participate fully in their communities. Supports a network of specialist projects that run programmes of horticultural activity for training and employment, therapy and health. Provides expert advice on easier and accessible gardening for everyone, including older or mobility-restricted people.

t: 0118 988 5688   **e:** info@thrive.org.uk   **w:** www.thrive.org.uk

WOMEN'S ENVIRONMENTAL NETWORK

P.O Box 3062, London E1 1TZ

Women's perspective, advice and information on environmental issues. Their 'Cultivating the Future' project encourages networks food-growing initiatives amongst ethnic minority and disadvantaged women. Contact them for womens' allotment projects nationally.

t: 020 7481 9004   **e:** info@wen.org.uk   **w:** www.wen.org.uk

Publications

MAGAZINES

■ ALLOTMENT AND LEISURE GARDENER

The quarterly magazine of the N.S.A.L.G
www.nsalg.org.uk

■ AMATEUR GARDENER

It was the Allotments 2000 campaign run by this publication which helped to bring the allotments issue to Parliament – and form the 1998 Select Committee looking into The Future for Allotments. Contact: amateur_gardening@ipcmedia.com

■ EF! ACTION UPDATE

The magazine of the Earth First! Network. Find your local contact at: www.eco-action.org/efau

■ GARDENING WHICH

Very active in the field of allotments and community gardens.

Contact: 2 Marylebone Rd, London NW1 4DF

■ KITCHEN GARDEN
Available in good newsagents, this magazine is friendly to leisure and commercial smallholdings, and a source of growing information.
Contact: www.kitchengarden.co.uk

■ PERMACULTURE MAGAZINE
Full of interesting articles about things sustainable - from gardening to alternative energy
w: www.permaculture.co.uk

■ PERMACULTURE NEWS
The organ of the Permaculture Association - great source of general information and listings for permaculture and other courses.
e: office@permaculture.org.uk   **w:** www.permaculture.org.uk

■ SCHNEWS
Weekly newsheet of the alternative and direct action movement- full of forthcoming events and news which doesn't make the mainstream.
w: www.cbuzz.co.uk/schnews/index.html

BOOKS

■ ACCESSIBLE GARDENING
J. Woy
Tip and techniques for making your plot accessible to the elderly and disabled

■ ACTIVISTS GUIDE TO THE MEDIA
by George Monbiot. Land Is Ours website
Useful insider's look at the media for campaigners and activists.

■ ACTIVISTS GUIDE TO THE PLANNING SYSTEM
Land is Ours website
Everything you need to know. I have cribbed some of it for this book. Hard copy available from The Land Is Ours.

■ THE ALLOTMENT: ITS LANDSCAPE AND CULTURE
by David Crouch and Colin Ward, Five Leaves Press
This book explores the culture and landscape of the allotment and the part it has played in Britain for 150 years.

■ THE ART OF ALLOTMENTS
D. Crouch, 5 Leaves Press
Lots of ideas for artistic ways to celebrate your own plot. Fun book.

■ BACK GARDEN SEED-SAVING

by Sue Stickland, eco-logic books

Latest book on seed saving, includes lots of practical information and vegetable varieties. Chapter on starting a local seed saving network

■ BACKYARD COMPOSTING

by J Roulac, Green Books

Good cheap book on composting

■ COMMON GROUND BOOK OF ORCHARDS

ed by Common Ground

The only book on community orchards – beautifully produced, full of relevant information.

■ COMPLETE FUNDRAISING HANDBOOK

by Sam Clarke and Michael Norton, Directory of Social Change

Everything you need to know about fundraising. Fund-raisers' bible.

■ COMPOSTING WITH WORMS

by G. Pilkington, eco-logic books

Convert allotment waste to soil enhancing compost.

■ DEFINING RURAL SUSTAINABILITY

Chapter 7

15 criteria for Sustainable Developments in the Countryside together with Three Model Policies for Local Plans. Useful for sustainability ideas within a model setting of sustainable land use and management.

■ *ENCYCLOPEDIA OF GREEN WOODWORKING

by Ray Tabor, eco-logic books

The book to get if you want to make fences, hurdles, benches etc from green wood found on or near your site.

■ ENVIRONMENTAL FUNDING GUIDE

Directory of Social Change

Chock full of details of environmental funders.

■ FACILTATOR'S GUIDE TO PARTICIPATORY DECISION MAKING

by Sam Kaner

Essential for those who want an end to inconclusive or divisive meetings.

■ FOREST GARDENING

by Robert Hart, Green Books

The classic book on forest gardening.

■ GERRARD WINSTANLEY AND THE REPUBLIC OF HEAVEN

Dales Historical Monographs, Cumbria

A good all round introduction to the man and his thought.

■ GERRARD WINSTANLEY: SELECTED WRITINGS

ed. Andrew Hopton, Aporia Press

■ **GROWING IN THE COMMUNITY: A GOOD PRACTICE GUIDE FOR THE MANAGEMENT OF ALLOTMENTS**
by David Crouch, Joe Sempik and Richard Wiltshire, LGA Publications
Essential guide for all those who manage allotments, or who want to know what those who manage them should be thinking.

■ **GROWING ORGANIC ANNUAL 2000**
Bradford Community Environment Project
Celebrating the growing achievements of Bradford and District Schools, Nurseries and other food growing projects in Bradford.

■ **GROWING UNUSUAL VEGETABLES**
by Simon Hickmott, eco-logic books
A source of interesting vegetables with full growing instructions, many commonly grown by Caribbean and Asian communities.

■ **HDRA LEAFLETS**
● Crash Course on flying pests ● Gardening manures for organic soil improvement ● Grow your own organic fruit - getting started
● Grow your own organic vegetables - getting started ● Growing food on a budget ● Growing organic herbs ● On the trail of the slug
● Organic soil care ● Organic weed control ●l Starting an organic allotment

■ **HOW TO MAKE A FOREST GARDEN**
by P. Whitefield, Permanent Publications
Good practical guide to making forest gardens

■ **HOW TO STOP AND INFLUENCE PLANNING PERMISSION**
by Speer and Dade
Valuable guide to working with your local planning system.

■ **HOW TO GROW MORE VEGETABLES THAN YOU EVER THOUGHT POSSIBLE ON LESS LAND...**
J. Jeavons, 10 Speed Press
American but the best book on getting the most out of your raised beds

■ **JUSTIS CD ROM**
Context Electronic Publishers
A full electronic, cross-referenced library of all UK legal statutes. Available for use in all main libraries and universities.

■ **LAW OF ALLOTMENTS**
by J F Garner
Useful trawl through allotments legislation. Available from libraries.

■ **MANAGING FOR CHANGE**
by A Davies
How to run community projects

■ **MEDIATORS HANDBOOK**
by J. Beer, New Society Publishers
Does what it says on the label.

■ **ORGANIC GARDENING**
by Stickland & Pears, RHS
Best of the bunch of basic organic gardening books

■ **PERMACULTURE GARDEN**
by G Bell, Harper Collins
Best book on Permaculture gardening

■ **PLANTS FOR A FUTURE**
by K Fearn, Permanent Publications
Chock full of useful and unusual plants.

■ **PLANTS FOR A FUTURE DATABASE**
Plants for a Future
Fully-searchable database of more than 7,000 useful plants.

■ **POWER IN OUR HANDS**
by Tony Gibson, Jon Carpenter
Wonderful, empowering book for local activists and world shakers.

■ **SEED SAVERS HANDBOOK**
by J Cherfas and M & J Fenton, eco-logic books,
Everything you needed to know about seed saving but were afraid to ask.

■ **SUSTAINABLE COMMUNITIES IN THE 21ST CENTURY**
A Government document designed to help councils who have not yet started the LA21 process.

■ **THIS LAND IS OUR LAND**
by Marion Shoard, Gaia Publications
The book to read for all those interested in land rights in Britain.

■ **VALUABLE VEGETABLES**
by Mandy Pullen, eco-logic books
Invaluable for those with larger areas to cultivate, good sections on selling surplus vegetables. Fast becoming a classic growers text.

■ **WRITING BETTER FUNDRAISING APPLICATIONS**
Directory of Social Change
When you know everything, put it to the test with this book.

Many of these books can be ordered from eco-logic books
www.eco-logicbooks.com

DIGNITY STATEMENT

There are many different kinds of people who take up tenancies on allotment sites within the Borough of Reigate and Banstead.

This diversity reflects the richness of the community and the wealth of different ideas and customs that improves the experience of each individual.

Reigate and Banstead Borough Council aims to ensure that all who enjoy the allotments will be treated with dignity, respect and equity – by staff, Councillors, Stewards and by each other.

Distinctions based on any of the following will not be tolerated:

Gender	Race	Nationality
Ethnic identity	National origin	Status
Role in the community	Religious or political beliefs	Disability
Age	Marital status	Family circumstance
Sexual orientation		

Harassment; bullying; intimidation; aggression; rudeness; ridicule; insulting, foul or obscene language; insulting, foul or obscene gestures, will not be tolerated under any circumstances. Anyone who is found to be breaking these rules will be required to give up their allotment plot.

This policy will be implemented and monitored by officers of Reigate and Banstead Borough Council and by the Stewards of the allotment sites, taking as standard behaviour that which would be considered acceptable to a reasonable person.

If you wish to make a complaint about a matter covered by this statement please telephone 01737 276119 and you will be told what you need to do to take the matter further. You may be a witness or you may feel this is happening to you. Remember that we will protect your right to enjoy your allotment free of any prejudice, interference or insult.

MODEL CONSTITUTION for an ALLOTMENT ASSOCIATION

1 - NAME

The _____ Allotment Association

2 - OBJECTIVES

(1) To promote the interests of allotment holders and to take joint action for the benefit of members.

(2) To co-operate with any committee set up by the government, local authorities and other bodies, to further the interests of allotment holders.

(3) To cooperate with any committee, local authority, national or local body set up to provide seeds, potatoes, tools, etc. for allotment holders.

(4) To take whatever steps required with the local authority for the good management and cultivation of allotment gardens.

(5) To protect members from damage, trespass and theft, where possible.

(6) To approve the appointment of Trustees for the _____ Allotment Site, as provided for by any lease between the Association and _____ Council or its successors.

(7) To arrange lectures, film shows, demonstrations, competitions and other social events.

(8) To co-operate with other gardening associations in matters of mutual interest.

3 - MEMBERS

The Association shall consist of all persons who are current, legal, and paid-up holders of allotment gardens on the _____ Allotment Site, together with their spouses.

4 - SUBSCRIPTIONS

Every member shall pay an annual subscription, the amount of which will be decided by a General Meeting. Subscriptions will be payable in advance and as part of the overall rental payment for the member's allotment garden.

5 - OFFICERS

The Officers shall be a Chairman, Treasurer and Secretary, who shall be ex-officio members of the Committee. They shall be elected at each Annual General Meeting. Retiring Officers shall be eligible for re-election.

6 - COMMITTEE

The affairs of the Association will be conducted by a Committee of Management of not less than 8 members, each of whom may serve as a Trustee for the _____ Allotment Site, as provided for by any lease between the Association and _____ City Council or its successors. The Committee will retire at the Annual General Meeting but will be eligible for re-election. Casual vacancies shall be filled by the Committee and the members so appointed shall hold office until the next Annual General Meeting. A quorum at Committee meetings shall be not less than 5 members.

7 - GENERAL MEETINGS

The Annual General Meeting, of which seven days' notice shall be given and at which the audited accounts and Secretary's report shall be submitted and the officers for the ensuing year elected. If a Special General Meeting is necessary, it must be called by a minimum of ten members at Committee or a General Meeting. Ten members shall form a quorum, and in the case of equal voting the Chair shall have a casting vote. Voting shall be on the basis of one vote per allotment holder, irrespective of the number of plots cultivated. Members will be notified in advance of any proposed changes to the constitution, which will be discussed and voted on at a General Meeting.

8 -

No party-political or sectarian discussions shall be raised or resolutions proposed at either Committee or General Meeting.

9 - FUNDS

The Committee shall open a banking account in the name of the Association and all monies received from any source on behalf of the Association shall be paid into such account. Cheques shall be signed by two out of three signatories. Association funds will not be spent by the Committee other than to pay rent for any lease between the Association and the _____ City Council or its successors, or unless it directly benefits allotment holders on the site.

10 - AUDIT

There shall be appointed an Auditor, who is not a member of the Committee, to audit the accounts and submit a Report to the Annual General Meeting.

ON YOUR HEADED NOTEPAPER
PRESS RELEASE
Embargoed: Wednesday 11 March 2005

OURTOWN COUNCIL ACCUSED OF HYPOCRISY AND ARROGANCE AS LOCALS FIGHT TO SAVE GREEN OASIS

Ourtown Council's self-proclaimed green credentials being questioned after it issued an eviction order that will lead to the destruction of a local green oasis. The battle between the council and local allotment holders began when Ourtown Council ordered that a former bomb site in Yourdale Road, near Newington Green, be vacated within three months to make way for a new building development. However, planning' applications have not been received and local residents have not been consulted. The site has been an allotment for the past 15 years.

Ourtown Council makes much of its concern for the environment and says it operates green policies including:

● ensuring the protection of current open spaces; recycling existing buildings rather than building on open space; returning empty properties to interim/permanent use; encouraging local food production.

All these appear to be contradicted by Ourtown's extraordinary decision to destroy the Yourdale Road allotment. Jane White of Ourtown Allotment Society said:

"We are extremely upset by Ourtown Council's plans to destroy the allotment in Yourdale Road. We support the need to build houses and facilities for the community on brownfield rather than greenfield sites, and there is so much derelict and unused land in Ourtown, we can't understand why they want to destroy this much-used green oasis. If the council goes ahead with this decision its concerns for the environment will be little more than green hypocrisy.

"Ourtown Council's astonishing arrogance in evicting us without issuing planning permission or consulting local residents has only made us resolve to fight even harder. We are not going to quietly let the council take away something that has given so my people so much pleasure – the battle has only just begun."

ENDS

More Information: Jane White   XXXX XXX XXX (h)
                  Nigel Blue   XXXX XXX X (w) XXXX XX (m)

ON YOUR HEADED NOTEPAPER
PRESS RELEASE
Immediate Release: 30 June 1998

CHAIR OF COMMONS ENVIRONMENT COMMITTEE APPLAUDS DECISION TO SAVE OURTOWN ALLOTMENTS

Ourtown residents are celebrating victory after a cross-party consensus saved four allotments from being sold to a housing association for development last night (9 June).

Labour, Lib-Dems and Greens voted against the disposal of the site – at Springdale Rd – which had been on the cards since a decision was taken before May's local elections. Last night's meeting at Ourtown Town Hall was expected to rubber stamp the recommendation to sell the site. However, not only has the allotment been saved but the Council has promised to introduce an allotments policy in line with the recommendations of the Commons Environment Committee which has just reported on the future of allotments in England.

Ourtown Allotment Society were thrilled with the decision. "Common sense has triumphed and a precious urban growing site has been saved," said Jane White a spokesperson for the Society. "We are delighted, and applaud the Council's decision to introduce an allotments policy in the Ourtown, which is long overdue and in line with the Council's Agenda 21 commitments."

Roger Green MP, chair of the Commons Environment, Transport and Regions Committee said: "I am absolutely delighted to hear that the argument for retaining the allotments prevailed. There is no doubt in my mind that allotments are an extremely valuable asset for any local authority. I hope this will be start of many such victories for allotment holders up and down the country."

Liberal Democrat Cllr Helen Black, who moved the amendment said: "It was my concern about the over-development of my ward which pushed me into moving the amendment. These plots are a little green oasis in a heavily congested area."

Officers have now been charged to actively seek alternative sites for the housing association.

ENDS

For more information tel: XXXX XXX XXX

Reproduced by kind permission of Pete Loveday

eco-logic books

eco-logic books is a small, ethically-run company that specialises in publishing and distributing books and other material that promote practical solutions to environmental problems.

Those books that are still in print and mentioned in the Further Reading List plus many others are available from our comprehensive catalogue. Other topics covered in the catalogue include:

Gardening
Permaculture
Composting
Self Reliance
Food and related Issues
Keeping Hens and other Domestic Animals
Smallholding & Farming
Wildlife
Trees, Woodland Crafts & Forestry
Orchards and Fruit Growing
Community
Building & Construction
Alternative Energy
Urban issues
Transport
Money and the Economy
Trade Skills
Sustainabilty
Radical Thinking
Managing for Change

A FREE mail order catalogue can be downloaded in a couple of minutes from the web or send a large s.a.e. to the address below:

eco logic books
10 -12 Picton Street, Bristol BS6 5QA, England
Tel: 0117 942 0165 Fax: 0117 942 0164
email: books@eco-logicbooks.com   web: www.eco-logicbooks.com